LESSON PLANNING FOR PRIMARY SCHOOL TEACHERS

WITH 500 PLANNING IDEAS

DR DHEERAJ MEHROTRA

Contents

Preface

Lesson planning is at the heart of effective teaching, especially in primary school settings, where young minds are shaped and nurtured. **"Lesson Planning for Primary School Teachers"** is designed to provide educators with a comprehensive collection of 500 creative and adaptable lesson planning ideas that can enhance students' learning experience. This book aims to support teachers in delivering engaging, structured, and meaningful lessons while fostering a stimulating environment where every student's learning style is considered.

The foundation of a child's educational journey is laid in the primary years, making it crucial for teachers to deliver lessons that are not only informative but also dynamic and fun. This book emphasizes the importance of varied teaching strategies, encouraging educators to approach each subject with fresh perspectives that keep students intrigued and excited. Whether through group activities, hands-on projects, or multimedia tools, these lesson plans offer opportunities to make learning interactive, comprehensive, and accessible.

This resource, designed to inspire creativity and flexibility, caters to primary school teachers' unique challenges. It provides a wide range of lesson ideas for various subjects, including language arts, mathematics, science, and social studies. Each lesson plan is thoughtfully organized to ensure it meets learning objectives, addresses diverse student needs, and promotes active participation.

As teachers, we understand that the classroom is a dynamic space, constantly evolving to meet the needs of all students. These lesson plans can help teachers create environments that foster curiosity, growth, and a love for learning. Whether you're a new teacher seeking guidance or an experienced educator looking for fresh ideas, this book will be invaluable in your teaching journey.

We hope this collection of lesson plans inspires you to design memorable and impactful learning experiences that will resonate with your students for years to come.

www.authordheerajmehrotra.com

ONE
IMPORTANCE OF LESSON PLANNING

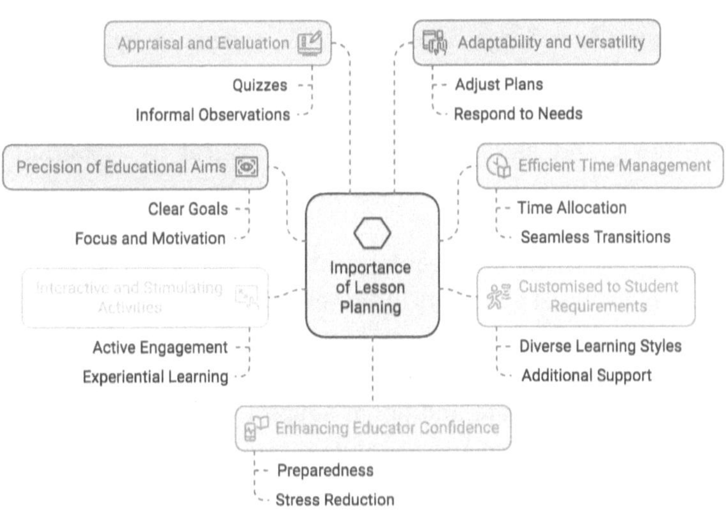

Friends, Lesson planning is crucial for elementary education since it offers educators a systematic framework to convey knowledge efficiently while promoting an engaging and inclusive learning atmosphere. Pupils cultivate core abilities at the primary level, and meticulously designed lessons can substantially improve their educational experience. Several fundamental factors underscore the importance of lesson planning in basic education:

1. Precision of Educational Aims

An explicit lesson plan delineates the learning objectives for each session, guaranteeing that both educators and learners comprehend the expectations. When educators establish explicit, quantifiable goals, pupils can learn their required achievements more effectively. This clarity aids primary pupils in maintaining focus and motivation.

2. Efficient Time Management

Effective time management is essential for sustaining engagement with young children. Lesson preparation enables educators to decompose knowledge into digestible segments, guaranteeing comprehensive coverage of crucial topics without inundating the pupils. Planning encompasses time allocation for activities, transitions, and assessments, which is critical in sustaining a seamless and organised classroom atmosphere.

3. Customised to Student Requirements

Lesson plans assist educators in addressing the varied requirements of primary children. This encompasses varied instructional tactics to accommodate diverse learning styles and capabilities. Some pupils may necessitate additional support, although others may gain from advanced materials or solo tasks. Planning allows the educator to adequately address these needs, ensuring all kids can participate and learn.

4. Interactive and Stimulating Activities

Elementary school pupils acquire knowledge most effectively when they engage actively in their education. Lesson preparation enables educators to create engaging, interactive, and experiential activities.

A structured class, whether utilising games, collaborative tasks, or creative activities, guarantees student engagement while repeating essential concepts. This form of learning is particularly vital for young children, who may possess diminished attention spans.

5. Appraisal and Evaluation

An effectively organised class plan incorporates assessment tools, like quizzes, talks, or informal observations. This formative exam enables educators to evaluate comprehension and pinpoint areas requiring additional attention for primary children. Monitoring student progress and delivering essential feedback becomes challenging without a lesson plan.

6. Adaptability and Versatility

While lesson plans offer a definitive framework, they also permit adaptability. Educators can adjust plans in response to students' reactions, conduct, or unforeseen obstacles. A robust plan establishes a basis, yet it may be modified to accommodate the changing requirements of the class. This versatility is especially crucial in a primary school when student demands can change swiftly.

7. Enhancing Educator Confidence

Lesson planning fosters confidence in both novice and seasoned educators. Well-prepared instructors are more inclined to feel in command of the classroom and assured in managing any circumstance. The planning process enables educators to foresee challenges, fostering a sense of readiness and alleviating stress.

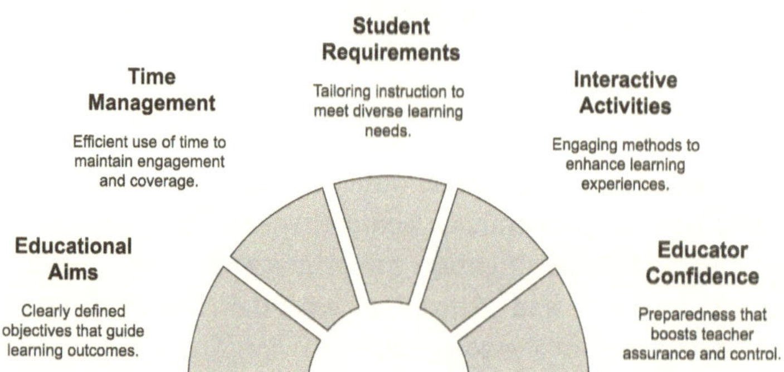

Lesson Planning
Student Requirements
Tailoring instruction to meet diverse learning needs.
Time Management
Efficient use of time to maintain engagement and coverage.
Interactive Activities
Engaging methods to enhance learning experiences.
Educational Aims
Clearly defined objectives that guide learning outcomes.
Educator Confidence
Preparedness that boosts teacher assurance and control.

TWO

500 Lesson Planning Ideas

Here, we randomly discuss some lesson plans for various subjects of interest for classroom teachers.

1. English Language

Topic: "Introduction to Adjectives"

- **Objective:** Students will identify adjectives and use them in sentences.
- **Activity:** Students bring a favorite object to class and describe it using at least three adjectives.
- **Assessment:** Write three sentences using adjectives in their journals.

2. Mathematics

Topic: "Introduction to Fractions"

- **Objective:** Students will understand the concept of fractions as parts of a whole.
- **Activity:** Use a pizza model to demonstrate halves, quarters, and thirds.
- **Assessment:** Students divide a paper circle into different fractions.

3. Science
Topic: "Plant Growth and Needs"

- **Objective:** Students learn about sunlight, water, and soil for plant survival.
- **Activity:** Plant seeds in small cups and monitor growth.
- **Assessment:** Record changes in a plant journal.

4. Social Studies
Topic: "My Community Helpers"

- **Objective:** Students will identify various community helpers and their roles.
- **Activity:** Role-play as different community helpers.
- **Assessment:** Complete a matching worksheet of helpers and their tools.

5. Art & Craft
Topic: "Collage Creation"

- **Objective:** Students express creativity by making a collage using paper scraps.
- **Activity:** Theme-based collage (e.g., seasons or festivals).
- **Assessment:** Explain their artwork to peers.

The Multifaceted Benefits of Lesson Planning

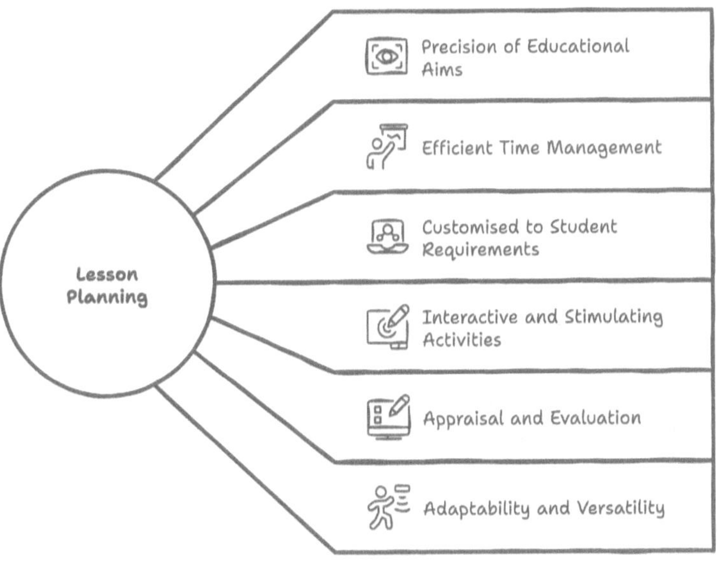

6. Physical Education
Topic: "Teamwork Games"

- **Objective:** Develop teamwork and coordination.
- **Activity:** Play a relay race emphasising team collaboration.
- **Assessment:** Reflect on the experience in a group discussion.

1. **Topic:** Story Sequencing

   - **Objective:** Arrange the events of a story in order.
   - **Activity:** Use a familiar fairy tale and provide cut-out story cards.
   - **Assessment:** Students arrange the cards and narrate the story.

2. **Topic:** Rhyming Words

   - **Objective:** Identify and create rhyming words.
   - **Activity:** Rhyming bingo game with picture cards.
   - **Assessment:** Students write rhymes for given words.

3. **Topic:** Creative Writing

   - **Objective:** Write a short story based on a picture prompt.
   - **Activity:** Provide a picture and guide brainstorming sessions.
   - **Assessment:** Students read stories aloud.

4. **Topic:** Vocabulary Building

   - **Objective:** Learn new words related to a theme (e.g., animals).
   - **Activity:** Create a word web with drawings.
   - **Assessment:** Use words in sentences.

Mathematics

1. **Topic:** Time Telling

   - **Objective:** Read analog clocks for the hour and half hours.
   - **Activity:** Use toy clocks for practice.
   - **Assessment:** Complete worksheets with clock diagrams.

2. **Topic:** Skip Counting

   - **Objective:** Count by 2s, 5s, and 10s.
   - **Activity:** Hopscotch numbers activity.
   - **Assessment:** Solve skip-counting problems on paper.

3. **Topic:** Money Recognition

   - **Objective:** Identify and count coins.
   - **Activity:** Play a shopping game with fake currency.
   - **Assessment:** Correctly count and match money amounts.

Science

8. **Topic:** Water Cycle

   - **Objective:** Explain evaporation, condensation, and precipitation.
   - **Activity:** Draw the water cycle and label parts.
   - **Assessment:** Oral explanation.

9. **Topic:** Animal Habitats

   - **Objective:** Match animals to their habitats.
   - **Activity:** Habitat sorting game with pictures.
   - **Assessment:** Complete a matching worksheet.

10. **Topic:** States of Matter

- **Objective:** Understand solids, liquids, and gases.
- **Activity:** Group objects into categories.
- **Assessment:** Identify states of matter from everyday items.

Social Studies

11. **Topic:** National Symbols

- **Objective:** Recognize and name symbols of the country.
- **Activity:** Coloring sheets of flags and emblems.
- **Assessment:** Quiz on symbols.

12. **Topic:** Community Rules

- **Objective:** Understand the importance of rules in society.
- **Activity:** Create a classroom rules chart.
- **Assessment:** Role-play scenarios with rule-following.

Arts and Creativity

13. **Topic:** Color Mixing

- **Objective:** Learn primary and secondary colors.
- **Activity:** Mix paints to create new colors.
- **Assessment:** Paint a picture using mixed colors.

14. **Topic:** Origami Basics

- **Objective:** Fold paper to create shapes.
- **Activity:** Make simple origami animals.
- **Assessment:** Display creations.

Physical Education

15. **Topic:** Balancing and Coordination

- **Objective:** Develop balance skills.
- **Activity:** Walk on a low beam or line.
- **Assessment:** Perform balancing tasks successfully.

16. **Topic:** Team Games

- **Objective:** Foster collaboration and communication.
- **Activity:** Tug-of-war.
- **Assessment:** Reflect on team strategies.

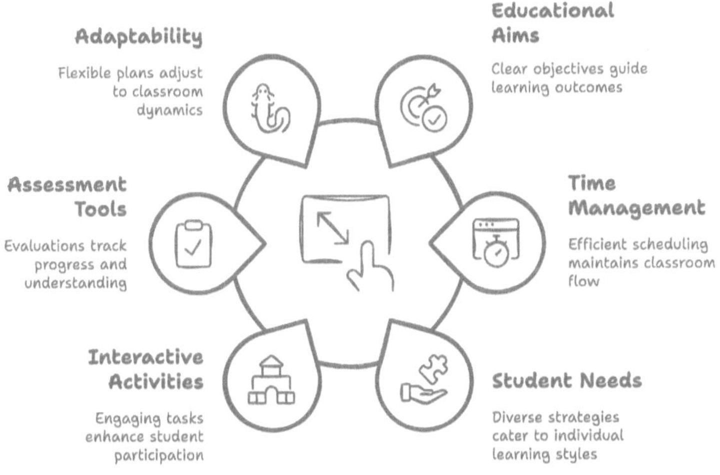

Language Arts

17. **Topic:** Poetry Appreciation

- **Objective:** Identify rhyming words and express feelings through poetry.
- **Activity:** Recite a simple poem and create a class poem together.
- **Assessment:** Share their favorite line from the poem.

18. **Topic:** Role-Playing Characters

- **Objective:** Enhance comprehension by acting out a story.
- **Activity:** Assign story roles and conduct a play.
- **Assessment:** Participation and understanding of character motivations.

19. **Topic:** Synonyms and Antonyms

- **Objective:** Understand and use synonyms and antonyms.
- **Activity:** Word matching game using flashcards.
- **Assessment:** Use words in sentences.

Mathematics

20. **Topic:** Shapes Around Us

- **Objective:** Identify geometric shapes in daily life.
- **Activity:** Shape scavenger hunt in the classroom.
- **Assessment:** Draw and label the shapes found.

21. **Topic:** Simple Addition and Subtraction

- **Objective:** Solve addition and subtraction problems.
- **Activity:** Use number lines and manipulatives like beads.
- **Assessment:** Complete practice problems on a worksheet.

22. **Topic:** Measuring Length

- **Objective:** Understand units of measurement.
- **Activity:** Measure classroom items with a ruler.
- **Assessment:** Record measurements in a table.

Science

23. **Topic:** Healthy Eating

- **Objective:** Understand the food pyramid.
- **Activity:** Create a balanced meal using magazine cutouts.
- **Assessment:** Present their meal to the class.

24. **Topic:** Seasons and Weather

- **Objective:** Identify characteristics of different seasons.
- **Activity:** Draw a tree in all four seasons.
- **Assessment:** Explain their drawing.

25. **Topic:** Plant Life Cycle

- **Objective:** Understand how plants grow.
- **Activity:** Plant seeds in small pots and observe growth.
- **Assessment:** Keep a plant diary.

Social Studies

26. **Topic:** Map Skills

- **Objective:** Identify continents and oceans.
- **Activity:** Complete a puzzle map of the world.
- **Assessment:** Label continents and oceans on a blank map.

27. **Topic:** Famous Leaders

- **Objective:** Learn about a historical figure.
- **Activity:** Create a mini-booklet about their life.
- **Assessment:** Share one interesting fact they learned.

Arts and Creativity

28. **Topic:** Collage Making

- **Objective:** Express creativity using mixed media.
- **Activity:** Create a collage based on a theme (e.g., nature).
- **Assessment:** Explain their collage to the class.

29. **Topic:** Musical Instruments

- **Objective:** Identify sounds and names of instruments.
- **Activity:** Create simple instruments using everyday items.
- **Assessment:** Perform a group rhythm.

Lesson Planning in Basic Education

Pros	VS	Cons
Clear objectives		Time-consuming
Time management		Rigidity
Customization		Over-preparation
Engaging activities		Stressful for teachers
Assessment tools		Potential for burnout

Physical Education

30. **Topic:** Fitness Challenge

- **Objective:** Improve motor skills.
- **Activity:** Complete a simple obstacle course.
- **Assessment:** Reflect on the activity in a group discussion.

31. **Topic:** Team Collaboration

- **Objective:** Work effectively as a team.
- **Activity:** Play cooperative games like relay races.
- **Assessment:** Evaluate teamwork and communication.

Values and Life Skills

32. **Topic:** Empathy Building

- **Objective:** Recognize and respect others' feelings.
- **Activity:** Read a story about kindness and discuss it.
- **Assessment:** Create a kindness pledge.

33. **Topic:** Problem-Solving Skills

- **Objective:** Learn to solve conflicts amicably.
- **Activity:** Act out conflict scenarios and propose solutions.
- **Assessment:** Reflect on the scenarios.

34. **Topic:** Listening Skills

- **Objective:** Improve focus and understanding through active listening.
- **Activity:** Listen to an audio story and answer comprehension questions.
- **Assessment:** Share key points from the story.

35. **Topic:** Creative Writing: Picture Prompts

- **Objective:** Encourage imagination and storytelling.
- **Activity:** Write a story based on a picture provided.
- **Assessment:** Evaluate creativity and structure.

Mathematics

36. **Topic:** Patterns and Sequences

- **Objective:** Identify and extend patterns.
- **Activity:** Use objects like beads to create color or shape patterns.
- **Assessment:** Complete pattern worksheets.

37. **Topic:** Basic Fractions

- **Objective:** Understand the concept of parts of a whole.
- **Activity:** Use paper pizzas to show halves, quarters, and thirds.
- **Assessment:** Solve fraction problems.

Science

38. **Topic:** Animal Habitats

- **Objective:** Learn about different animal homes.
- **Activity:** Match animals to their habitats using flashcards.
- **Assessment:** Draw and label an animal in its habitat.

39. **Topic:** Magnets and Their Uses

- **Objective:** Understand magnetic properties.
- **Activity:** Conduct experiments to see what items a magnet attracts.
- **Assessment:** Create a list of magnetic and non-magnetic items.

Social Studies

40. **Topic:** Community Helpers

   - **Objective:** Recognize roles of community workers.
   - **Activity:** Dress up as a community helper and explain their job.
   - **Assessment:** Peer discussion about their chosen helper.

41. **Topic:** National Symbols

   - **Objective:** Identify and understand the importance of national symbols.
   - **Activity:** Create a collage of national flags, animals, and emblems.
   - **Assessment:** Quiz on their meanings.

Arts and Creativity

42. **Topic:** Color Wheel

   - **Objective:** Learn primary and secondary colors.
   - **Activity:** Mix paints to discover new colors.
   - **Assessment:** Create a painting using all learned colors.

43. **Topic:** Origami Basics

   - **Objective:** Enhance fine motor skills through paper folding.
   - **Activity:** Make simple animals or objects using origami instructions.
   - **Assessment:** Display and describe their creations.

Physical Education

44. **Topic:** Balance and Coordination

- **Objective:** Develop motor control.
- **Activity:** Walk on a straight line carrying a beanbag on their head.
- **Assessment:** Self-reflect on the difficulty level.

45. **Topic:** Aerobics for Fun

- **Objective:** Improve cardiovascular health and energy levels.
- **Activity:** Follow a kid-friendly aerobic dance routine.
- **Assessment:** Participate actively in the session.

Language Arts

46. **Topic:** Synonyms and Antonyms

- **Objective:** Build vocabulary by understanding word relationships.
- **Activity:** Match synonyms and antonyms with flashcards.
- **Assessment:** Write sentences using paired words.

47. **Topic:** Poetry Appreciation

- **Objective:** Foster an interest in poetry.
- **Activity:** Read and analyze a simple poem, then write a four-line poem.
- **Assessment:** Evaluate creativity and rhyme schemes.

Mathematics

48. **Topic:** 2D Shapes

- **Objective:** Identify and describe geometric shapes.
- **Activity:** Create pictures using cut-outs of shapes.
- **Assessment:** Name the shapes used in their artwork.

49. **Topic:** Money and Transactions

- **Objective:** Learn basic currency and its value.
- **Activity:** Simulate a shopping experience with play money.
- **Assessment:** Role-play as a cashier and buyer, calculating totals and change.

Science

50. **Topic:** Plant Life Cycle

- **Objective:** Explore the stages of plant growth.
- **Activity:** Plant seeds and observe their growth over weeks.
- **Assessment:** Document observations in a journal.

51. **Topic:** Types of Rocks

- **Objective:** Classify rocks based on appearance and texture.
- **Activity:** Create a mini rock collection and categorize them.
- **Assessment:** Explain rock types in a presentation.

Social Studies

52. **Topic:** Festivals Around the World

- **Objective:** Understand cultural diversity.
- **Activity:** Research a festival and present it to the class.
- **Assessment:** Peer evaluations on presentations.

53. **Topic:** Map Skills

- **Objective:** Learn to read basic maps.
- **Activity:** Identify landmarks on a school or community map.
- **Assessment:** Create a map of their neighborhood.

Arts and Creativity

54. **Topic:** Exploring Textures

- **Objective:** Identify and use different materials to create art.
- **Activity:** Make a collage using fabric, paper, and natural elements.

- **Assessment:** Discuss their choice of materials.

55. **Topic:** Cartoon Character Drawing

   - **Objective:** Develop drawing skills.
   - **Activity:** Use grids to replicate cartoon images.
   - **Assessment:** Display their completed drawing.

Physical Education

56. **Topic:** Team Games: Relay Races

   - **Objective:** Build teamwork and coordination.
   - **Activity:** Organize a relay race with simple rules.
   - **Assessment:** Observe collaboration and participation.

57. **Topic:** Stretching Exercises

   - **Objective:** Learn basic stretching techniques.
   - **Activity:** Follow a guided stretching routine.
   - **Assessment:** Perform the stretches correctly.

Lesson Planning

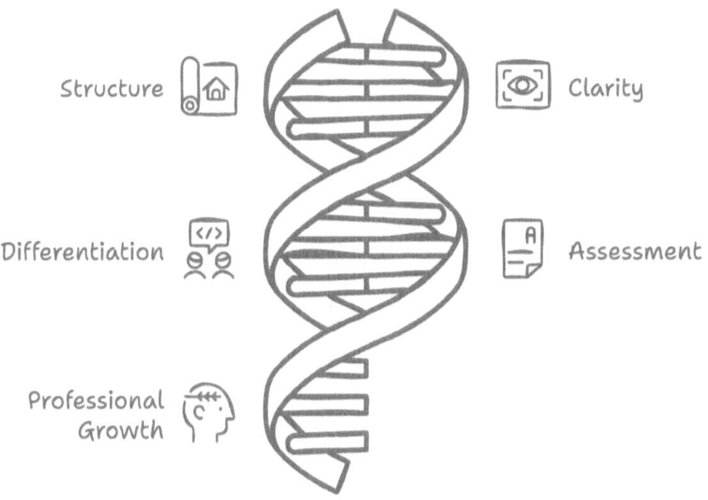

Language Arts

58. **Topic:** Story Sequencing

- **Objective:** Improve comprehension through sequencing events.
- **Activity:** Rearrange shuffled story cards in the correct order.
- **Assessment:** Retell the story orally or in writing.

59. **Topic:** Listening Skills

- **Objective:** Enhance active listening.
- **Activity:** Listen to a short story and answer questions about it.
- **Assessment:** Use a comprehension quiz based on the story.

Mathematics

60. **Topic:** Odd and Even Numbers

- **Objective:** Identify and sort numbers as odd or even.
- **Activity:** Use objects (e.g., pencils) for grouping and classification.
- **Assessment:** Solve a worksheet with sorting exercises.

61. **Topic:** Symmetry

- **Objective:** Understand lines of symmetry.
- **Activity:** Fold paper shapes to discover symmetrical lines.
- **Assessment:** Draw symmetrical lines for given figures.

Science

62. **Topic:** Properties of Water

- **Objective:** Explore states of water and their changes.
- **Activity:** Experiment with ice, water, and steam.

- **Assessment:** Discuss the observed changes in small groups.

63. **Topic:** Animal Habitats

   - **Objective:** Match animals to their correct habitats.
   - **Activity:** Create a habitat collage using pictures.
   - **Assessment:** Describe the needs of an animal in its habitat.

   Social Studies

64. **Topic:** Community Helpers

   - **Objective:** Recognize the roles of various community workers.
   - **Activity:** Role-play community helper professions.
   - **Assessment:** Write a thank-you note to a chosen helper.

65. **Topic:** Time and Timelines

   - **Objective:** Learn how events are organized chronologically.
   - **Activity:** Create a personal timeline.
   - **Assessment:** Present the timeline to classmates.

   Arts and Creativity

66. **Topic:** Origami Basics

   - **Objective:** Develop fine motor skills and creativity.
   - **Activity:** Fold simple origami designs (e.g., boats or animals).
   - **Assessment:** Display completed designs in class.

67. **Topic:** Puppet Making

   - **Objective:** Encourage storytelling through crafts.
   - **Activity:** Make hand or finger puppets from socks or paper.
   - **Assessment:** Perform a short story using their puppets.

Physical Education

68. **Topic:** Obstacle Courses

- **Objective:** Develop agility and problem-solving skills.
- **Activity:** Complete a fun, age-appropriate obstacle course.
- **Assessment:** Observe and discuss teamwork or strategies used.

69. **Topic:** Coordination Through Ball Games

- **Objective:** Enhance hand-eye coordination.
- **Activity:** Play catch with varying ball sizes.
- **Assessment:** Perform a simple accuracy test with targets.

Enhancing Teacher Effectiveness through Lesson Planning

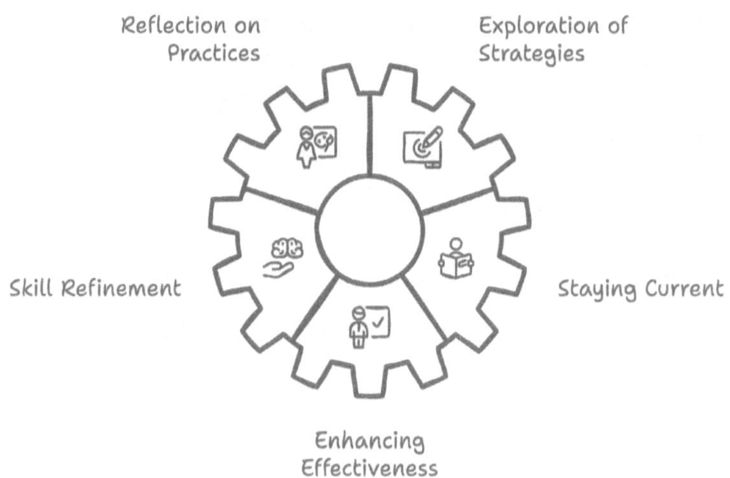

Language Arts

70. **Topic:** Word Families

   - **Objective:** Recognize patterns in word families to enhance reading.
   - **Activity:** Create a word tree with words from a specific family (e.g., *-at*).
   - **Assessment:** Group words by their families during an interactive game.

71. **Topic:** Writing Simple Sentences

   - **Objective:** Form sentences using given words.
   - **Activity:** Arrange word cards into meaningful sentences.
   - **Assessment:** Write original sentences in a notebook.

Mathematics

72. **Topic:** Measuring Length

   - **Objective:** Understand how to measure using rulers and non-standard units.
   - **Activity:** Measure classroom objects and record findings.
   - **Assessment:** Solve a worksheet requiring length comparisons.

73. **Topic:** Patterns and Sequences

   - **Objective:** Identify and create repeating patterns.
   - **Activity:** Use colored beads or paper shapes to design a sequence.
   - **Assessment:** Identify the next item in a given pattern.

Science

74. **Topic:** Magnetism

- **Objective:** Explore magnetic and non-magnetic objects.
- **Activity:** Test classroom items with a magnet and record observations.
- **Assessment:** Group objects into magnetic or non-magnetic categories.

75. **Topic:** The Water Cycle

- **Objective:** Understand the stages of the water cycle.
- **Activity:** Create a water cycle diagram with labels and arrows.
- **Assessment:** Match water cycle terms with their correct definitions.

Social Studies

76. **Topic:** Flags Around the World

- **Objective:** Identify and learn the significance of national flags.
- **Activity:** Draw and color a flag and present its importance.
- **Assessment:** Match flags to their respective countries.

77. **Topic:** Cultural Celebrations

- **Objective:** Appreciate diverse traditions and holidays.
- **Activity:** Share stories or items related to personal cultural celebrations.
- **Assessment:** Create a class chart of celebrations with descriptions.

Arts and Creativity

78. **Topic:** Creative Collages

- **Objective:** Express creativity using a mix of materials.
- **Activity:** Make a theme-based collage (e.g., nature, seasons).

- **Assessment:** Explain the theme and elements in their collage.

79. **Topic:** Drama and Role-Play

- **Objective:** Build confidence through performance.
- **Activity:** Act out a scene from a favorite story.
- **Assessment:** Peer feedback on clarity and expression.

Physical Education

80. **Topic:** Balance and Coordination

- **Objective:** Develop motor skills through fun exercises.
- **Activity:** Walk on a marked line or beam.
- **Assessment:** Time students and track progress.

81. **Topic:** Group Activities

- **Objective:** Foster teamwork and communication.
- **Activity:** Play a cooperative game like "Pass the Ball Without Dropping."
- **Assessment:** Discuss strategies for better teamwork.

Language Arts

82. **Topic:** Picture Descriptions

- **Objective:** Develop speaking and vocabulary skills.
- **Activity:** Show students a picture and ask them to describe it in complete sentences.
- **Assessment:** Peer feedback and class discussion.

83. **Topic:** Rhyming Words

- **Objective:** Identify and create rhyming pairs.

- **Activity:** Play a rhyming word-matching game.
- **Assessment:** Write a short poem with rhyming lines.

Mathematics

84. **Topic:** Time Management

- **Objective:** Understand hours, minutes, and seconds.
- **Activity:** Practice setting times on analogue clocks.
- **Assessment:** Solve a worksheet with time-related problems.

85. **Topic:** Geometry Basics

- **Objective:** Identify 2D shapes and their properties.
- **Activity:** Create art using geometric shapes.
- **Assessment:** Match shapes to their descriptions.

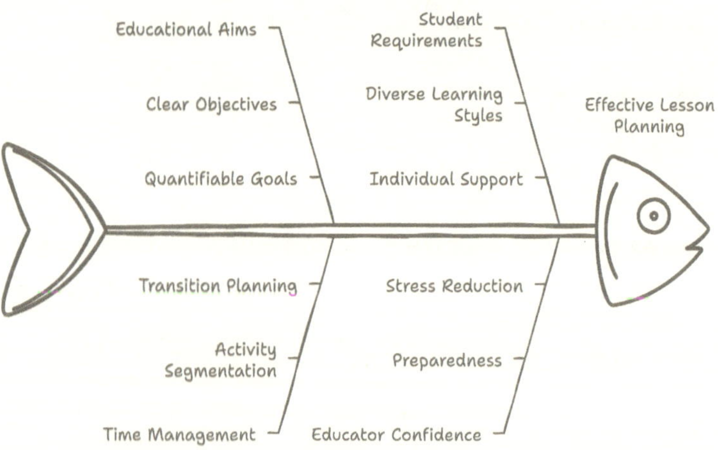

Science

86. **Topic:** Plant Life Cycle

   - **Objective:** Learn the stages of plant growth.
   - **Activity:** Observe a plant growing from seed over weeks.
   - **Assessment:** Draw and label a plant life cycle chart.

87. **Topic:** Sound and Vibrations

   - **Objective:** Understand how sound is produced.
   - **Activity:** Create simple instruments like rubber band guitars.
   - **Assessment:** Explain how their instrument produces sound.

Social Studies

88. **Topic:** Local Government

   - **Objective:** Understand the roles of local officials.
   - **Activity:** Role-play a town meeting with assigned roles.
   - **Assessment:** Write a reflection on their role in the activity.

89. **Topic:** Historical Landmarks

   - **Objective:** Learn about famous landmarks.
   - **Activity:** Create a postcard for a landmark.
   - **Assessment:** Present their postcards to the class.

Arts and Creativity

90. **Topic:** Exploring Texture

   - **Objective:** Identify and use textures in art.

- **Activity:** Create a textured artwork using materials like fabric or leaves.
- **Assessment:** Discuss the textures used and their effects.

91. **Topic:** Music and Movement

- **Objective:** Express emotions through movement.
- **Activity:** Move to different styles of music and discuss how it feels.
- **Assessment:** Perform a short movement piece to a chosen song.

Physical Education

92. **Topic:** Fitness Fun

- **Objective:** Understand the importance of exercise.
- **Activity:** Rotate through exercise stations like jumping jacks or hula hoops.
- **Assessment:** Reflect on their favourite station and why.

93. **Topic:** Relay Races

- **Objective:** Develop teamwork and physical endurance.
- **Activity:** Participate in a variety of relay races.
- **Assessment:** Discuss strategies to improve performance.

Language Arts

94. **Topic:** Building Sentences

- **Objective:** Understand sentence structure.
- **Activity:** Provide word cards for students to create sentences.
- **Assessment:** Identify subjects and predicates in sentences.

95. **Topic:** Listening Skills

- **Objective:** Improve active listening abilities.
- **Activity:** Read a short story and ask comprehension questions.
- **Assessment:** Answer reflective questions about the story.

Mathematics

96. **Topic:** Patterns and Sequences

- **Objective:** Recognize and complete patterns.
- **Activity:** Create patterns with coloured blocks.
- **Assessment:** Solve pattern-based worksheets.

97. **Topic:** Measurement

- **Objective:** Use tools to measure length.
- **Activity:** Measure classroom objects using rulers or tape measures.
- **Assessment:** Record measurements in a chart.

Science

98. **Topic:** Animal Habitats

- **Objective:** Learn about various habitats.
- **Activity:** Match animals to their habitats using flashcards.
- **Assessment:** Create a habitat diorama.

99. **Topic:** Properties of Water

- **Objective:** Observe water's states and behaviour.
- **Activity:** Experiment with ice melting and water evaporation.
- **Assessment:** Discuss observations and write conclusions.

Social Studies

100. **Topic:** Community Helpers

- **Objective:** Learn about the roles of community helpers.
- **Activity:** Role-play different jobs in the community.
- **Assessment:** Share which helper role they liked most and why.

101. **Topic:** Cultural Celebrations

- **Objective:** Understand diverse traditions.
- **Activity:** Research and present at a global festival.
- **Assessment:** Create a poster showcasing key aspects of the festival.

Arts and Creativity

102. **Topic:** Collage Creation

- **Objective:** Use mixed media to create art.
- **Activity:** Create collages using magazine cutouts and other materials.
- **Assessment:** Share their work and describe the theme.

103. **Topic:** Exploring Music Genres

- **Objective:** Identify characteristics of different music genres.
- **Activity:** Listen to samples and categorize them.
- **Assessment:** Discuss how the genres make them feel.

Physical Education

104. **Topic:** Yoga for Kids

- **Objective:** Learn basic yoga poses for relaxation.
- **Activity:** Practice poses like tree, cat, and cobra.
- **Assessment:** Reflect on how yoga made them feel.

105. **Topic:** Throwing and Catching

- **Objective:** Develop hand-eye coordination.
- **Activity:** Partner activities with soft balls.
- **Assessment:** Record accuracy over several trials.

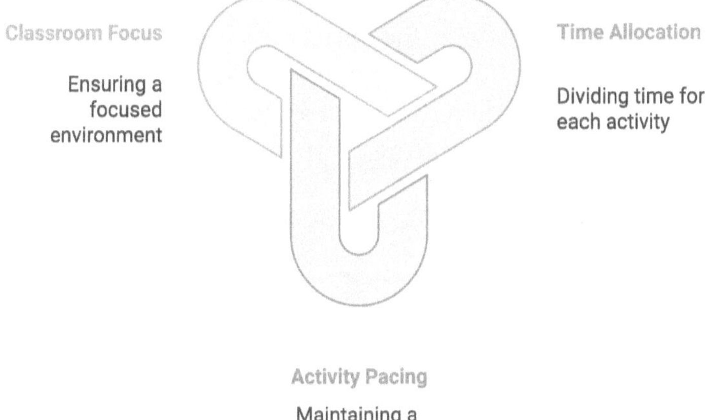

Language Arts

106. **Topic:** Story Retelling

- **Objective:** Improve narrative sequencing skills.
- **Activity:** Read a story aloud and ask students to retell it in their own words.
- **Assessment:** Evaluate retellings for inclusion of main events.

107. **Topic:** Letter Writing

- **Objective:** Understand the structure of formal and informal letters.
- **Activity:** Write a letter to a friend or family member.
- **Assessment:** Check for correct format and clarity.

Mathematics

108. **Topic:** Exploring Shapes

- **Objective:** Identify 2D and 3D shapes.
- **Activity:** Shape hunt in the classroom.
- **Assessment:** Create a chart listing objects and their corresponding shapes.

109. **Topic:** Comparing Numbers

- **Objective:** Use more significant than, less than, and equal to signs.
- **Activity:** Solve number comparison puzzles.
- **Assessment:** Complete a worksheet with mixed comparison exercises.

Science

110. **Topic:** Food Chains

   - **Objective:** Understand the flow of energy in ecosystems.
   - **Activity:** Create a food chain diagram for a specific habitat.
   - **Assessment:** Present the diagram to the class.

111. **Topic:** Weather Patterns

   - **Objective:** Recognize and describe different weather types.
   - **Activity:** Keep a weather diary for a week.
   - **Assessment:** Discuss how weather changes impact daily life.

   Social Studies

112. **Topic:** Map Skills

   - **Objective:** Read and interpret maps.
   - **Activity:** Identify landmarks on a local map.
   - **Assessment:** Draw a simple map of the classroom.

113. **Topic:** Historical Figures

   - **Objective:** Learn about key historical personalities.
   - **Activity:** Research a historical figure and present findings.
   - **Assessment:** Create a fact file about the chosen figure.

   Arts and Creativity

114. **Topic:** Symmetry in Art

   - **Objective:** Create symmetrical designs.
   - **Activity:** Use paint to make butterfly prints.
   - **Assessment:** Share and explain how symmetry was achieved.

115. **Topic:** Exploring Textures

- **Objective:** Use textures in creative work.
- **Activity:** Make texture rubbings using crayons and textured surfaces.
- **Assessment:** Create a collage using rubbings.

Physical Education

116. **Topic:** Teamwork Challenges

- **Objective:** Foster collaboration through physical tasks.
- **Activity:** Complete obstacle courses in teams.
- **Assessment:** Reflect on what made teamwork successful.

117. **Topic:** Balancing Acts

- **Objective:** Develop balance and coordination.
- **Activity:** Practice balancing on beams or with props.
- **Assessment:** Demonstrate improvement in balance over time.

Language Arts

118. **Topic:** Understanding Synonyms and Antonyms

- **Objective:** Expand vocabulary using synonyms and antonyms.
- **Activity:** Create a chart of common words and their opposites.
- **Assessment:** Use new words in sentences.

119. **Topic:** Descriptive Writing

- **Objective:** Enhance descriptive writing skills.
- **Activity:** Write a description of a favorite place.
- **Assessment:** Evaluate use of sensory details.

Mathematics

120. **Topic:** Time and Clocks

  - **Objective:** Understand time concepts and tell time.
  - **Activity:** Practice reading analog and digital clocks.
  - **Assessment:** Complete a worksheet with time-related problems.

121. **Topic:** Patterns and Sequences

  - **Objective:** Recognize and create patterns.
  - **Activity:** Create patterns using colors or shapes.
  - **Assessment:** Identify patterns in everyday objects.

Science

122. **Topic:** The Water Cycle

  - **Objective:** Understand the process of the water cycle.
  - **Activity:** Create a water cycle model using household materials.
  - **Assessment:** Explain the steps of the water cycle.

123. **Topic:** Plant Growth

  - **Objective:** Learn the conditions needed for plant growth.
  - **Activity:** Grow a plant in the classroom and observe changes.
  - **Assessment:** Keep a growth journal and track changes.

Social Studies

124. **Topic:** Community Helpers

  - **Objective:** Learn about different roles in the community.
  - **Activity:** Create a collage of community helpers.
  - **Assessment:** Present the roles of selected helpers.

125. **Topic:** National Symbols

- **Objective:** Recognize national symbols and their significance.
- **Activity:** Create a booklet with national symbols.
- **Assessment:** Explain the meaning of each symbol.

Arts and Creativity

126. **Topic:** Color Mixing

- **Objective:** Learn primary and secondary colours.
- **Activity:** Mix primary colours to create secondary colours.
- **Assessment:** Identify colours made from the mixing activity.

127. **Topic:** Collage Making

- **Objective:** Explore creativity through collage art.
- **Activity:** Create a collage using different materials.
- **Assessment:** Present the finished collage with an explanation.

Physical Education

128. **Topic:** Coordination and Reflexes

- **Objective:** Improve hand-eye coordination and reflexes.
- **Activity:** Play reflex games like balloon keep-up.
- **Assessment:** Evaluate improvement in reflex speed.

129. **Topic:** Jumping Skills

- **Objective:** Develop jumping and agility skills.
- **Activity:** Conduct long jump or high jump activities.
- **Assessment:** Measure and track progress.

Language Arts

130. **Topic:** Rhyming Words

- **Objective:** Identify and create rhyming words.
- **Activity:** Read rhyming poems and identify pairs.
- **Assessment:** Have students write their rhyming poem.

131. **Topic:** Sentence Structure

   - **Objective:** Understand the structure of a simple sentence.
   - **Activity:** Create sentences using a subject, verb, and object.
   - **Assessment:** Identify parts of the sentence in a class exercise.

   Mathematics

132. **Topic:** Money and Coins

   - **Objective:** Learn to identify and count different coins.
   - **Activity:** Set up a mock store and practice buying and selling.
   - **Assessment:** Use different coins to make specific amounts.

133. **Topic:** Simple Addition and Subtraction

   - **Objective:** Practice essential addition and subtraction.
   - **Activity:** Use objects or flashcards for addition/subtraction games.
   - **Assessment:** Solve word problems using basic operations.

   Science

134. **Topic:** Animals and Their Habitats

   - **Objective:** Understand the relationship between animals and their habitats.
   - **Activity:** Create a habitat diorama for a selected animal.
   - **Assessment:** Present the habitat with details about the animal.

135. **Topic:** Seasons and Weather

- **Objective:** Learn about different seasons and weather patterns.
- **Activity:** Keep a weather journal for a week.
- **Assessment:** Classify activities for different seasons.

Social Studies

136. **Topic:** Types of Houses Around the World

- **Objective:** Explore different types of houses in various cultures.
- **Activity:** Create a presentation of house types from different countries.

Language Arts

137. **Topic:** Synonyms and Antonyms

- **Objective:** Learn and use synonyms and antonyms.
- **Activity:** Word matching games with synonyms and antonyms.
- **Assessment:** Create a sentence using each word and its opposite.

138. **Topic:** Nouns and Pronouns

- **Objective:** Understand the difference between nouns and pronouns.
- **Activity:** Replace nouns with appropriate pronouns in sentences.
- **Assessment:** Have students fill in the blanks with the correct pronouns.

Mathematics

139. **Topic:** Patterns and Sequences

- **Objective:** Recognize patterns and create sequences.
- **Activity:** Use coloured shapes to make repeating patterns.

- **Assessment:** Have students create their pattern sequences.

140. **Topic:** Measurement

- **Objective:** Understand and practice measuring lengths.
- **Activity:** Measure classroom objects using rulers or measuring tapes.
- **Assessment:** Solve real-life problems involving measurement.

Science

141. **Topic:** Simple Machines

- **Objective:** Learn about simple machines (lever, pulley, etc.).
- **Activity:** Build a simple machine using everyday objects.
- **Assessment:** Identify simple machines around the classroom.

142. **Topic:** Plant Growth

- **Objective:** Understand how plants grow and the factors that affect growth.
- **Activity:** Grow a plant in the classroom and track its growth.
- **Assessment:** Write observations and draw the stages of growth.

Social Studies

143. **Topic:** Community Helpers

- **Objective:** Identify different roles in the community.
- **Activity:** Invite a community helper to speak with the class.
- **Assessment:** Students draw and explain the role of a community helper.

144. **Topic:** Landforms

- **Objective:** Learn about different landforms (mountains, rivers, etc.).
- **Activity:** Create a 3D map showing different landforms.
- **Assessment:** Have students label landforms on a map.

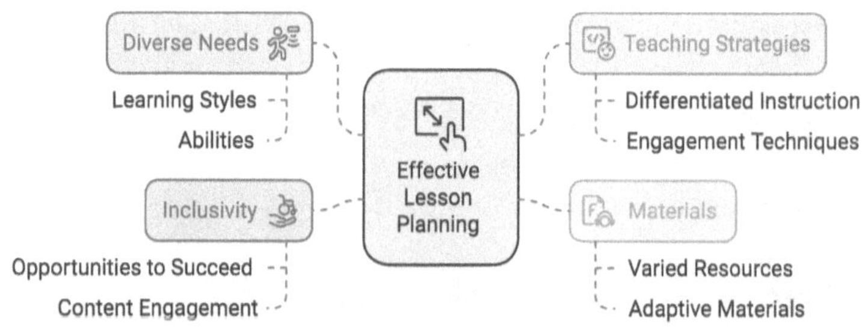

Language Arts

145. **Topic:** Rhyming Words

- **Objective:** Recognize and create rhyming words.
- **Activity:** Rhyming word match-up games.
- **Assessment:** Create a poem using at least five pairs of rhyming words.

146. **Topic:** Reading Comprehension

- **Objective:** Improve reading comprehension.
- **Activity:** Read a short passage and answer questions.
- **Assessment:** Create a set of questions based on the reading passage.

147. **Topic:** Adjectives

- **Objective:** Learn to describe nouns using adjectives.
- **Activity:** Use flashcards to match adjectives to nouns.
- **Assessment:** Write sentences using descriptive adjectives.

Mathematics

148. **Topic:** Addition and Subtraction

- **Objective:** Solve simple addition and subtraction problems.
- **Activity:** Use objects or counters to demonstrate addition and subtraction.
- **Assessment:** Solve ten addition and ten subtraction problems on paper.

149. **Topic:** Time

- **Objective:** Learn to read clocks and understand time.

- **Activity:** Use analogue and digital clocks for time-telling practice.
- **Assessment:** Set different times on a clock and ask students to read them.

150. **Topic:** Fractions

- **Objective:** Understand basic fractions (1/2, 1/4, etc.).
- **Activity:** Use paper folding or visual aids to explain fractions.
- **Assessment:** Color in fractions of a shape.

151. **Topic:** Multiplication

- **Objective:** Learn multiplication tables up to 10.
- **Activity:** Practice multiplication with flashcards or games.
- **Assessment:** Write out the multiplication tables up to 10.

Science

152. **Topic:** Water Cycle

- **Objective:** Understand the stages of the water cycle.
- **Activity:** Create a visual model of the water cycle.
- **Assessment:** Have students explain the process of the water cycle.

153. **Topic:** Living and Non-living Things

- **Objective:** Identify the characteristics of living and non-living things.
- **Activity:** Sort objects into living and non-living categories.
- **Assessment:** Students list five examples of each.

154. **Topic:** Solar System

- **Objective:** Learn about the planets and the solar system.
- **Activity:** Create a model or draw the solar system.
- **Assessment:** Write facts about each planet.

155. **Topic:** Animals and Their Habitats

- **Objective:** Learn where different animals live.
- **Activity:** Match animals to their habitats.
- **Assessment:** Describe the habitat of a chosen animal.

Social Studies

156. **Topic:** National Holidays

- **Objective:** Learn about the significance of national holidays.
- **Activity:** Discuss and create a poster of national holidays.
- **Assessment:** Write a paragraph about one holiday.

157. **Topic:** Transportation

- **Objective:** Learn about different modes of transportation.
- **Activity:** Discuss and draw various transportation methods.
- **Assessment:** Classify transportation into land, air, and water.

158. **Topic:** My Family

- **Objective:** Learn about family structures.
- **Activity:** Draw a family tree.
- **Assessment:** Share and describe their family members.

Art and Craft

159. **Topic:** Color Mixing

- **Objective:** Understand primary and secondary colours.

- **Activity:** Mix primary colours to create secondary colours.
- **Assessment:** Color a picture using primary and secondary colours.

160. **Topic:** Paper Tole Craft

- **Objective:** Learn the art of paper layering.
- **Activity:** Create a 3D picture using layered paper.
- **Assessment:** Present their paper tole craft.

161. **Topic:** Collage Making

- **Objective:** Create artwork by glueing different materials together.
- **Activity:** Make a collage using coloured paper, fabric, etc.
- **Assessment:** Discuss the materials used in the collage.

Physical Education

162. **Topic:** Jumping and Hopping

- **Objective:** Improve balance and coordination.
- **Activity:** Set up an obstacle course for jumping and hopping.
- **Assessment:** Perform a jumping or hopping challenge.

163. **Topic:** Teamwork Games

- **Objective:** Foster teamwork and collaboration.
- **Activity:** Play relay races or tug-of-war.
- **Assessment:** Reflect on how teamwork helped complete the activity.

Music

164. **Topic:** Rhythm and Beats

- **Objective:** Understand basic rhythm and beats.
- **Activity:** Clap hands or tap feet to a rhythmic pattern.
- **Assessment:** Perform a rhythm pattern in front of the class.

165. **Topic:** Musical Instruments

- **Objective:** Learn about different musical instruments.
- **Activity:** Show and tell about various instruments.
- **Assessment:** Name and describe three musical instruments.

Life Skills

166. **Topic:** Time Management

- **Objective:** Learn how to manage time effectively.
- **Activity:** Create a weekly timetable for schoolwork and play.
- **Assessment:** Discuss the importance of following a timetable.

167. **Topic:** Personal Hygiene

- **Objective:** Understand the importance of personal hygiene.
- **Activity:** Discuss hygiene habits and demonstrate proper handwashing.
- **Assessment:** Create a hygiene poster.

Language Arts

168. **Topic:** Alphabet Recognition

- **Objective:** Recognize and identify letters of the alphabet.
- **Activity:** Sing the alphabet song and match letters to objects.
- **Assessment:** Write out the alphabet in order.

169. **Topic:** Sentence Formation

- **Objective:** Learn to form simple sentences.
- **Activity:** Use word cards to form complete sentences.
- **Assessment:** Write and read three simple sentences aloud.

Mathematics

170. **Topic:** Shapes and Their Properties

- **Objective:** Identify basic shapes and understand their properties.
- **Activity:** Use paper cutouts to identify and sort shapes.
- **Assessment:** Draw a picture using at least three different shapes.

171. **Topic:** Measurement

- **Objective:** Learn to measure length, weight, and volume.
- **Activity:** Use a ruler to measure classroom objects.
- **Assessment:** Measure and record the length of five objects.

Science

172. **Topic:** Plant Growth

- **Objective:** Learn the stages of plant growth.
- **Activity:** Plant a seed and observe its growth over time.
- **Assessment:** Keep a journal of the plant's growth.

173. **Topic:** Sound and Hearing

- **Objective:** Understand how sound is produced and how we hear.
- **Activity:** Experiment with different materials to produce sounds.
- **Assessment:** Identify and list sounds heard in the environment.

Social Studies

174. **Topic:** Community Helpers

- **Objective:** Learn about different roles in a community.
- **Activity:** Discuss community helpers and their responsibilities.
- **Assessment:** Draw a picture of a community helper and write a sentence about their job.

175. **Topic:** Maps and Directions

- **Objective:** Understand how to read simple maps and follow directions.
- **Activity:** Create a simple map of the classroom and give directions.
- **Assessment:** Follow a map to locate a specific object.

Art and Craft

176. **Topic:** Color Mixing

- **Objective:** Learn to mix primary colours to create new ones.
- **Activity:** Mix paint to make secondary colours.
- **Assessment:** Paint a picture using primary and secondary colours.

177. **Topic:** Collage Art

- **Objective:** Create artwork using different materials.
- **Activity:** Cut out shapes from coloured paper to make a collage.
- **Assessment:** Explain the materials and shapes used in their collage.

Physical Education

178. **Topic:** Balancing Skills

- **Objective:** Improve balancing skills.
- **Activity:** Walk along a balance beam or a straight line on the floor.
- **Assessment:** Perform a balancing challenge for 10 seconds.

179. **Topic:** Team Sports

- **Objective:** Learn the importance of teamwork in sports.
- **Activity:** Play a group game like soccer or basketball.
- **Assessment:** Reflect on how teamwork made the game better.

Music

180. **Topic:** Song and Dance

- **Objective:** Learn to sing a simple song with accompanying dance.
- **Activity:** Sing and perform a simple song with hand movements.
- **Assessment:** Perform the song for the class.

Life Skills

181. **Topic:** Conflict Resolution

- **Objective:** Learn strategies to resolve conflicts peacefully.
- **Activity:** Role-play different conflict scenarios.
- **Assessment:** Discuss what they learned about resolving conflicts.

182. **Topic:** Safety Rules

- **Objective:** Understand basic safety rules at school and home.
- **Activity:** Create a poster with safety rules.
- **Assessment:** Discuss one safety rule at home and one at school.

Effective Lesson Planning Pyramid

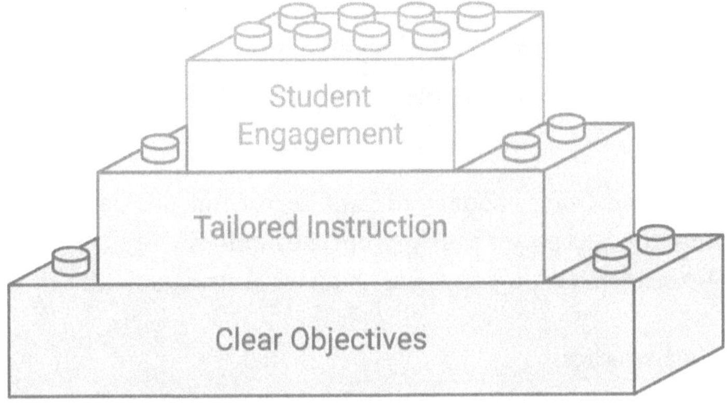

Language Arts

183. **Topic:** Rhyming Words

- **Objective:** Recognize and produce rhyming words.
- **Activity:** Read a poem and underline rhyming words.
- **Assessment:** Create a list of rhyming word pairs.

184. **Topic:** Word Families

- **Objective:** Learn about word families (e.g., cat, hat, bat).
- **Activity:** Sort words into appropriate families.
- **Assessment:** Write sentences using words from a family.

Mathematics

185. **Topic:** Place Value

- **Objective:** Understand the concept of place value for two-digit numbers.
- **Activity:** Use base-ten blocks to represent numbers.
- **Assessment:** Write and read numbers in expanded form.

186. **Topic:** Addition and Subtraction

- **Objective:** Add and subtract numbers within 100.
- **Activity:** Use number lines for addition and subtraction practice.
- **Assessment:** Solve problems on a worksheet.

Science

187. **Topic:** The Solar System

- **Objective:** Learn about the planets and their characteristics.
- **Activity:** Create a model of the solar system.

- **Assessment:** Write about one planet and its features.

188. **Topic:** Water Cycle

   - **Objective:** Understand the stages of the water cycle.
   - **Activity:** Draw and label the water cycle.
   - **Assessment:** Explain each stage of the water cycle.

Social Studies

189. **Topic:** Countries and Cultures

   - **Objective:** Learn about different countries and their cultures.
   - **Activity:** Research a country and present its culture.
   - **Assessment:** Share facts about the country's language, food, and traditions.

190. **Topic:** National Symbols

   - **Objective:** Understand the significance of national symbols.
   - **Activity:** Discuss and draw national symbols like the flag and national flower.
   - **Assessment:** Present the importance of the national symbols.

Art and Craft

191. **Topic:** Clay Modeling

   - **Objective:** Explore 3D art with clay.
   - **Activity:** Create simple figures or shapes using clay.
   - **Assessment:** Explain the process used to create the model.

192. **Topic:** Collage with Natural Materials

   - **Objective:** Create an art piece using natural materials.

- **Activity:** Collect leaves, twigs, and flowers for a collage.
- **Assessment:** Discuss how nature was used in the artwork.

Physical Education

193. **Topic:** Jumping and Landing

- **Objective:** Improve jumping and landing techniques.
- **Activity:** Practice jumping from different heights and landing safely.
- **Assessment:** Observe and correct their landing posture.

194. **Topic:** Relay Races

- **Objective:** Understand teamwork in relay races.
- **Activity:** Run a relay race in teams.
- **Assessment:** Discuss the importance of teamwork and timing in the race.

Music

195. **Topic:** Rhythm Patterns

- **Objective:** Recognize and repeat rhythmic patterns.
- **Activity:** Clap or tap along to different rhythm patterns.
- **Assessment:** Create and perform your rhythm pattern.

Life Skills

196. **Topic:** Time Management

- **Objective:** Learn how to manage time effectively.
- **Activity:** Create a simple schedule for daily activities.
- **Assessment:** Discuss how planning helps with managing time.

197. **Topic:** Healthy Eating

- **Objective:** Understand the importance of a balanced diet.
- **Activity:** Plan a healthy meal using food groups.
- **Assessment:** Discuss the benefits of eating healthy.

The Anatomy of Effective Lesson Planning

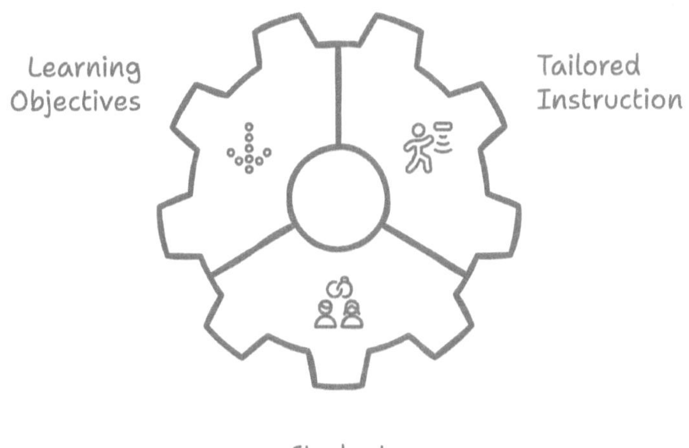

Language Arts

211. **Topic:** Sentence Structure

- **Objective:** Understand basic sentence construction.
- **Activity:** Create simple sentences using given words.
- **Assessment:** Rearrange words to form correct sentences.

212. **Topic:** Storytelling

- **Objective:** Develop storytelling skills.
- **Activity:** Students create and share their own stories.
- **Assessment:** Evaluate creativity and structure of stories.

Mathematics

213. **Topic:** Fractions

- **Objective:** Understand fractions as parts of a whole.
- **Activity:** Use objects like pizza or cake to demonstrate fractions.
- **Assessment:** Identify fractions in real-life scenarios.

214. **Topic:** Multiplication

- **Objective:** Understand basic multiplication concepts.
- **Activity:** Use multiplication charts to solve problems.
- **Assessment:** Solve word problems involving multiplication.

Science

215. **Topic:** Solar System

- **Objective:** Learn about planets and their characteristics.
- **Activity:** Create a model of the solar system.
- **Assessment:** Present facts about each planet.

216. **Topic:** Water Cycle

- **Objective:** Understand the stages of the water cycle.
- **Activity:** Create a water cycle diagram.
- **Assessment:** Explain each stage of the water cycle.

Social Studies

217. **Topic:** My Family

- **Objective:** Understand family roles and relationships.
- **Activity:** Create a family tree.
- **Assessment:** Present family trees to the class.

218. **Topic:** Geography of the Local Area

- **Objective:** Learn about local geography and landmarks.
- **Activity:** Explore a local map and identify key locations.
- **Assessment:** Write a short paragraph about a landmark.

Art and Craft

219. **Topic:** Collage Making

- **Objective:** Learn to make art with different materials.
- **Activity:** Create a collage using magazine cutouts and fabric.
- **Assessment:** Present the collage and explain the materials used.

220. **Topic:** Watercolor Painting

- **Objective:** Understand techniques of watercolour painting.
- **Activity:** Create a landscape painting using watercolours.
- **Assessment:** Evaluate creativity and use of colour.

Physical Education

221. **Topic:** Balance and Coordination

- **Objective:** Develop balance and coordination skills.
- **Activity:** Balance on one foot and perform various movements.
- **Assessment:** Observe and assess stability and coordination.

222. **Topic:** Group Relay Races

- **Objective:** Learn teamwork and improve running skills.
- **Activity:** Organize relay races in teams.
- **Assessment:** Evaluate team coordination and speed.

Music

223. **Topic:** Rhythm and Beat

- **Objective:** Understand rhythm and how to follow a beat.
- **Activity:** Clap and tap along with different rhythms.
- **Assessment:** Perform rhythms using instruments or clapping.

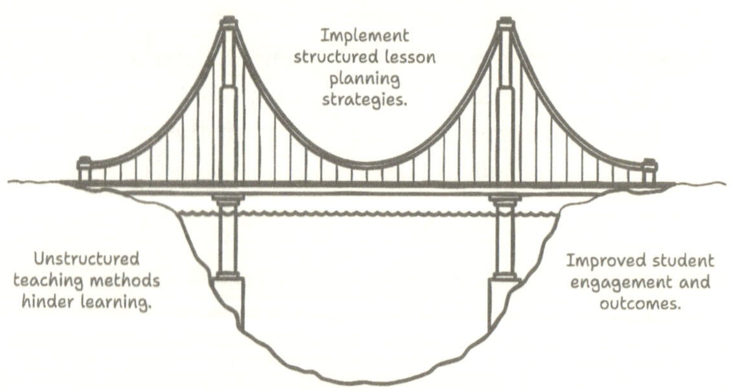

Language Arts

224. **Topic:** Alphabet Recognition

- **Objective:** Recognize and write uppercase and lowercase letters.
- **Activity:** Use flashcards to match letters with corresponding objects.
- **Assessment:** Identify letters in a given word.

225. **Topic:** Rhyming Words

- **Objective:** Identify and create rhyming words.
- **Activity:** Play a rhyming word game in pairs.
- **Assessment:** Write down five sets of rhyming words.

Mathematics

226. **Topic:** Counting and Number Recognition

- **Objective:** Recognize and count numbers up to 100.
- **Activity:** Use counting blocks or number charts.
- **Assessment:** Count aloud and identify numbers.

227. **Topic:** Simple Addition

- **Objective:** Understand basic addition concepts.
- **Activity:** Use objects like blocks to solve simple addition problems.
- **Assessment:** Solve fundamental addition problems.

Science

228. **Topic:** Plants and Growth

- **Objective:** Understand how plants grow and their parts.
- **Activity:** Plant seeds and observe their growth.
- **Assessment:** Draw and label parts of a plant.

229. **Topic:** Animals and Habitats

- **Objective:** Learn about various animals and where they live.
- **Activity:** Match animals to their habitats.
- **Assessment:** Write a paragraph about a chosen animal's habitat.

Social Studies

230. **Topic:** Community Helpers

- **Objective:** Understand the roles of people in a community.
- **Activity:** Discuss different jobs and their importance.
- **Assessment:** Create a poster of community helpers.

231. **Topic:** Seasons and Weather

- **Objective:** Learn about different seasons and their characteristics.
- **Activity:** Discuss the weather in different seasons.
- **Assessment:** Draw a picture representing each season.

Art and Craft

232. **Topic:** Paper Folding

- **Objective:** Learn the art of origami.
- **Activity:** Fold the paper to create basic shapes like cranes or boats.
- **Assessment:** Present the folded shapes to the class.

233. **Topic:** Clay Sculpting

- **Objective:** Understand the basics of sculpting with clay.
- **Activity:** Sculpt a small figure using modelling clay.
- **Assessment:** Evaluate creativity and technique.

Physical Education

234. **Topic:** Jumping Jacks and Stretching

- **Objective:** Improve flexibility and overall fitness.
- **Activity:** Perform jumping jacks and stretching exercises.
- **Assessment:** Evaluate physical performance and flexibility.

Music

235. **Topic:** Musical Instruments

- **Objective:** Recognize different types of musical instruments.
- **Activity:** Listen to sounds and match them with instruments.
- **Assessment:** Identify instruments from a sound clip.

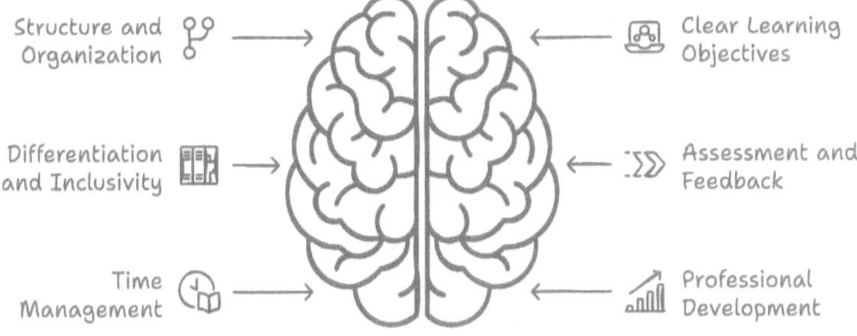

Language Arts

236. **Topic:** Identifying Nouns

- **Objective:** Understand and identify nouns in sentences.
- **Activity:** Highlight nouns in a short passage.
- **Assessment:** Identify five nouns from a given text.

237. **Topic:** Sentence Structure

- **Objective:** Learn how to form complete sentences.
- **Activity:** Arrange words to form meaningful sentences.
- **Assessment:** Write five sentences following the given structure.

Mathematics

238. **Topic:** Shapes and Geometry

- **Objective:** Recognize and name basic shapes.
- **Activity:** Draw and cut out basic shapes like squares, triangles, and circles.
- **Assessment:** Identify shapes in the classroom.

239. **Topic:** Number Patterns

- **Objective:** Understand and complete simple number patterns.
- **Activity:** Fill in the missing numbers in a sequence.
- **Assessment:** Create your number pattern for others to solve.

Science

240. **Topic:** Water Cycle

- **Objective:** Learn the stages of the water cycle.
- **Activity:** Use drawings and diagrams to explain the water cycle.

- **Assessment:** Label and describe the water cycle stages.

241. **Topic:** Solar System

- **Objective:** Identify planets in the solar system.
- **Activity:** Create a model or diagram of the solar system.
- **Assessment:** List all the planets and their characteristics.

Social Studies

242. **Topic:** Family and Relationships

- **Objective:** Understand different family structures and relationships.
- **Activity:** Draw a family tree.
- **Assessment:** Discuss the importance of family roles.

243. **Topic:** Celebrations Around the World

- **Objective:** Learn about different cultural celebrations.
- **Activity:** Discuss holidays like Diwali, Christmas, Eid, etc.
- **Assessment:** Prepare a presentation on a chosen celebration.

Art and Craft

244. **Topic:** Collage Making

- **Objective:** Learn to make a collage using various materials.
- **Activity:** Cut out pictures from magazines and create a collage.
- **Assessment:** Display and explain the collage's theme.

245. **Topic:** Watercolor Painting

- **Objective:** Introduce basic watercolour painting techniques.
- **Activity:** Paint a landscape using watercolours.

- **Assessment:** Evaluate creativity and technique in the artwork.

Physical Education

246. **Topic:** Throwing and Catching

- **Objective:** Improve hand-eye coordination.
- **Activity:** Practice throwing and catching a ball.
- **Assessment:** Measure accuracy and control.

Music

247. **Topic:** Tempo and Rhythm

- **Objective:** Understand the concept of tempo and rhythm.
- **Activity:** Clap along to different tempos of music.
- **Assessment:** Recognize slow, medium, and fast rhythms.

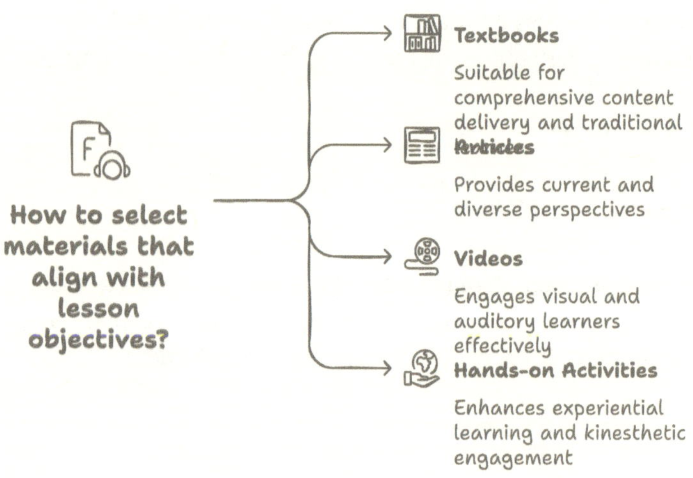

Science

248. **Topic:** Plant Life Cycle

- **Objective:** Understand the stages of plant growth.
- **Activity:** Plant a seed and observe its growth over time.
- **Assessment:** Draw a diagram of the plant life cycle.

249. **Topic:** Animals and Their Habitats

- **Objective:** Learn about different animal habitats.
- **Activity:** Match animals with their correct habitats.
- **Assessment:** Write about one animal and its habitat.

Language Arts

250. **Topic:** Rhyming Words

- **Objective:** Identify rhyming words in poems.
- **Activity:** Create a rhyming word list from a story.
- **Assessment:** Create a short poem with rhyming words.

251. **Topic:** Parts of Speech

- **Objective:** Identify nouns, verbs, adjectives, and pronouns in sentences.
- **Activity:** Label the parts of speech in a paragraph.
- **Assessment:** Write five sentences using different parts of speech.

Mathematics

252. **Topic:** Basic Addition and Subtraction

- **Objective:** Master simple addition and subtraction.

- **Activity:** Solve addition and subtraction word problems.
- **Assessment:** Complete a set of addition and subtraction problems.

253. **Topic:** Time

- **Objective:** Learn to read an analogue clock.
- **Activity:** Practice telling time with a clock.
- **Assessment:** Ask students to read the time at different hours.

Social Studies

254. **Topic:** Geography of India

- **Objective:** Learn about the states and capitals of India.
- **Activity:** Draw a map of India and label the states.
- **Assessment:** List the capitals of at least five states.

255. **Topic:** History of India

- **Objective:** Understand the ancient history of India.
- **Activity:** Discuss critical historical events in India.
- **Assessment:** Write a brief report on an ancient civilization.

Art and Craft

256. **Topic:** Drawing with Shapes

- **Objective:** Learn to use basic shapes to create a drawing.
- **Activity:** Create a picture using circles, squares, and triangles.
- **Assessment:** Present and describe the drawing.

257. **Topic:** Clay Modeling

- **Objective:** Develop fine motor skills through modeling.

- **Activity:** Create a simple object using clay.
- **Assessment:** Evaluate creativity and craftsmanship.

Physical Education

258. **Topic:** Jumping and Hopping

- **Objective:** Enhance coordination and balance.
- **Activity:** Jump over objects in a fun obstacle course.
- **Assessment:** Time the students and assess their balance.

Music

259. **Topic:** Understanding Musical Notes

- **Objective:** Learn to read introductory musical notes.
- **Activity:** Sing a song while following the notes on a chart.
- **Assessment:** Identify different notes on a musical staff.

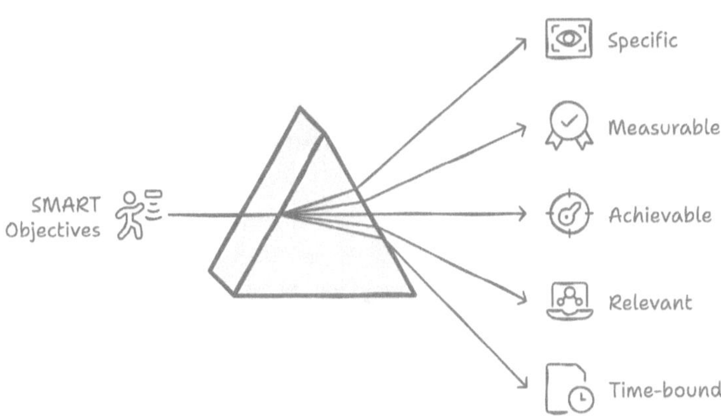

Mathematics

260. **Topic:** Shapes and Geometry

- **Objective:** Identify and classify different shapes.
- **Activity:** Create a collage using cut-out shapes.
- **Assessment:** Identify shapes in real-world objects.

261. **Topic:** Money and Shopping

- **Objective:** Understand the concept of currency and simple transactions.
- **Activity:** Set up a mock store and practice buying and selling.
- **Assessment:** Create a shopping list with prices and calculate totals.

Science

262. **Topic:** Weather Patterns

- **Objective:** Learn about different types of weather and how they occur.
- **Activity:** Keep a weather journal for a week and track daily changes.
- **Assessment:** Draw a chart of daily weather conditions.

263. **Topic:** Properties of Water

- **Objective:** Understand the physical properties of water.
- **Activity:** Perform experiments showing water in solid, liquid, and gas forms.
- **Assessment:** Write a report on the water cycle.

Language Arts

264. **Topic:** Writing Sentences

- **Objective:** Form complete sentences with correct structure.
- **Activity:** Build sentences using word cards.
- **Assessment:** Write five original sentences.

265. **Topic:** Vocabulary Development

- **Objective:** Learn new words and their meanings.
- **Activity:** Use a vocabulary book or app for daily practice.
- **Assessment:** Use new words in sentences.

Social Studies

266. **Topic:** Community Helpers

- **Objective:** Learn about people who help in the community.
- **Activity:** Interview a community helper or watch videos.
- **Assessment:** Write about how different helpers make the community better.

Physical Education

267. **Topic:** Balance and Coordination

- **Objective:** Develop physical balance and coordination.
- **Activity:** Play balance games such as "balance on one foot."
- **Assessment:** Observe the child's improvement in balancing skills.

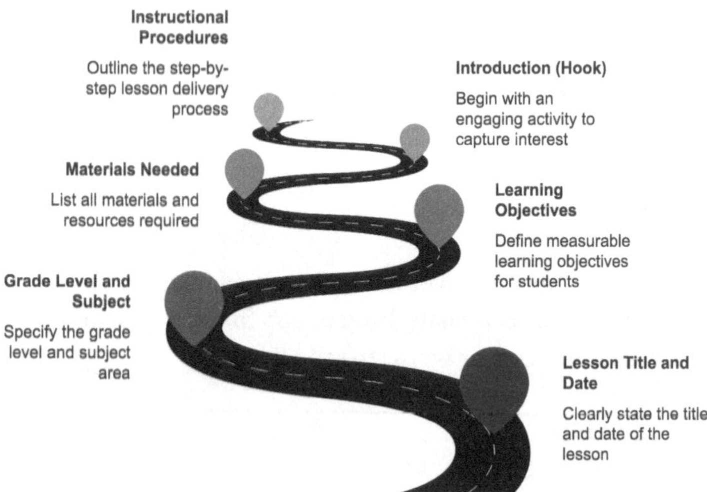

Lesson Plan Structure
Instructional Procedures
Outline the step-by-step lesson delivery process
Introduction (Hook)
Begin with an engaging activity to capture interest
Materials Needed
List all materials and resources required
Learning Objectives
Define measurable learning objectives for students
Grade Level and Subject
Specify the grade level and subject area
Lesson Title and Date
Clearly state the title and date of the lesson

Mathematics

268. **Topic:** Time and Clocks

- **Objective:** Learn how to read the time on an analogue clock.
- **Activity:** Practice setting the time on different clocks.
- **Assessment:** Ask students to tell the time from a clock face.

269. **Topic:** Simple Fractions

- **Objective:** Introduce fractions as part of a whole.
- **Activity:** Use paper folding to represent fractions.
- **Assessment:** Write fractions for different divided shapes.

Science

270. **Topic:** Plant Growth

- **Objective:** Understand how plants grow from seeds.
- **Activity:** Plant seeds and observe growth over weeks.
- **Assessment:** Record daily observations and discuss changes.

271. **Topic:** Light and Shadows

- **Objective:** Explore how light creates shadows.
- **Activity:** Use a flashlight to create shadows with different objects.
- **Assessment:** Ask students to draw objects with corresponding shadows.

Language Arts

272. **Topic:** Rhyming Words

- **Objective:** Identify and create rhyming words.

- **Activity:** Play rhyming word games with cards.
- **Assessment:** List five pairs of rhyming words.

273. **Topic:** Reading Comprehension

- **Objective:** Improve understanding of a short passage.
- **Activity:** Read a story aloud and discuss the main idea.
- **Assessment:** Answer simple questions related to the story.

Social Studies

274. **Topic:** Our Earth and Continents

- **Objective:** Identify the continents and oceans.
- **Activity:** Use a world map to point out continents.
- **Assessment:** Fill in a map with the names of continents.

Physical Education

275. **Topic:** Team Sports

- **Objective:** Learn teamwork and sportsmanship.
- **Activity:** Play a simple team sport like basketball or soccer.
- **Assessment:** Evaluate teamwork, communication, and participation.

Science

276. **Topic:** Weather and Seasons

- **Objective:** Understand different weather conditions and seasons.
- **Activity:** Create weather charts and track changes for a week.
- **Assessment:** Ask students to match weather conditions to the correct season.

277. **Topic:** States of Matter

   - **Objective:** Learn about solids, liquids, and gases.
   - **Activity:** Observe and classify everyday items into the three states.
   - **Assessment:** Have students describe examples of each state.

   Mathematics

278. **Topic:** Addition and Subtraction with Regrouping

   - **Objective:** Practice addition and subtraction using regrouping.
   - **Activity:** Solve problems with multi-digit numbers.
   - **Assessment:** Test students on solving word problems using these operations.

279. **Topic:** Measurement

   - **Objective:** Learn to measure length, weight, and volume.
   - **Activity:** Use rulers, scales, and measuring cups for practical exercises.
   - **Assessment:** Ask students to measure different objects in the classroom.

   Language Arts

280. **Topic:** Sentence Structure

   - **Objective:** Identify subjects and predicates in sentences.
   - **Activity:** Break down sentences and label each part.
   - **Assessment:** Students create their sentences using the structure.

281. **Topic:** Synonyms and Antonyms

- **Objective:** Learn synonyms and antonyms to enhance vocabulary.
- **Activity:** Play matching games with synonyms and antonyms.
- **Assessment:** Have students write sentences using synonyms and antonyms.

Social Studies

282. **Topic:** My Family and I

- **Objective:** Understand family roles and relationships.
- **Activity:** Create a family tree.
- **Assessment:** Ask students to present their family tree to the class.

Physical Education

283. **Topic:** Coordination and Agility

- **Objective:** Improve coordination and agility through exercises.
- **Activity:** Set up an obstacle course for students to complete.
- **Assessment:** Observe students' ability to complete the course.

Building Inspiring Learning Experiences

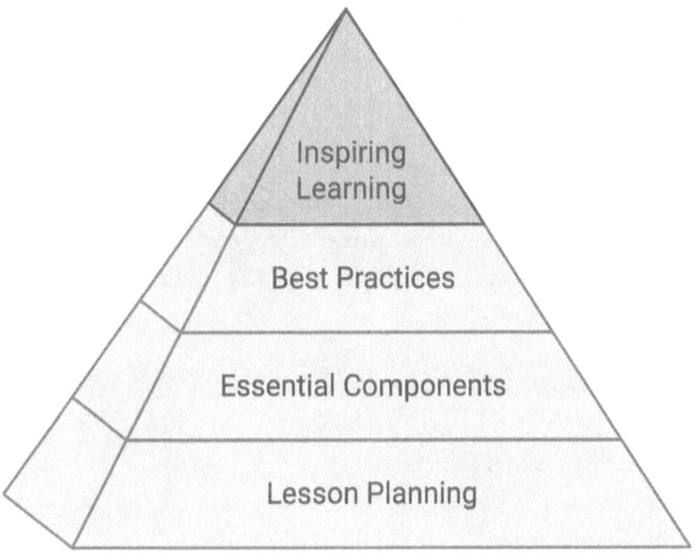

Science

284. **Topic:** Plants and Their Parts

- **Objective:** Identify the parts of a plant and their functions.
- **Activity:** Dissect a flower and label its parts.
- **Assessment:** Have students draw a plant and label its parts.

285. **Topic:** Simple Machines

- **Objective:** Understand types of simple machines and their uses.
- **Activity:** Create examples using pulleys and levers.
- **Assessment:** Ask students to identify simple machines in everyday objects.

Mathematics

286. **Topic:** Shapes and Geometry

- **Objective:** Recognize and name basic shapes.
- **Activity:** Shape scavenger hunt in the classroom or outdoors.
- **Assessment:** Students draw shapes and identify their properties.

287. **Topic:** Time – Reading Clocks

- **Objective:** Learn to read analogue and digital clocks.
- **Activity:** Use toy clocks to practice telling time.
- **Assessment:** Ask students to draw a clock showing specific times.

Language Arts

288. **Topic:** Rhyming Words

- **Objective:** Identify and create rhyming words.

- **Activity:** Play rhyming word games in groups.
- **Assessment:** Students create a poem with rhyming words.

289. **Topic:** Story Sequencing

- **Objective:** Understand the sequence of events in a story.
- **Activity:** Read a story and ask students to arrange events in order.
- **Assessment:** Students create their own story with a clear beginning, middle, and end.

Social Studies

290. **Topic:** Understanding Community Helpers

- **Objective:** Learn about the roles of different community helpers.
- **Activity:** Role-playing different community helpers.
- **Assessment:** Ask students to match jobs to the correct community helper.

Physical Education

291. **Topic:** Teamwork and Cooperation

- **Objective:** Encourage teamwork and cooperative skills.
- **Activity:** Organize team-building exercises like relay races.
- **Assessment:** Observe students' cooperation during activities.

Enhancing Lesson Planning

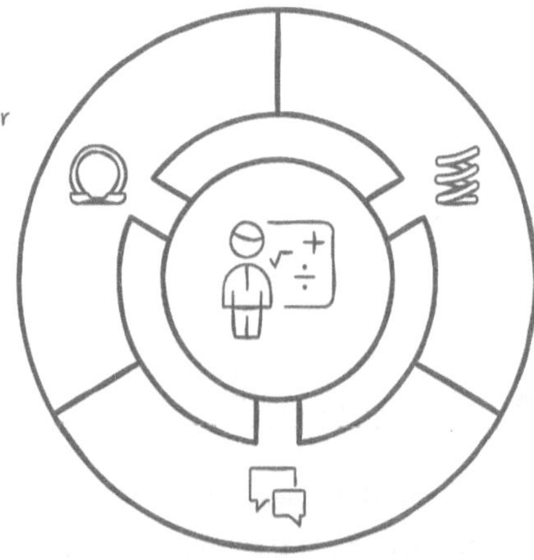

Science

292. **Topic:** Water Cycle

   - **Objective:** Understand the stages of the water cycle.
   - **Activity:** Create a simple water cycle model using a plastic bag.
   - **Assessment:** Students explain each stage of the water cycle.

293. **Topic:** Habitats and Animals

   - **Objective:** Identify different animal habitats and their features.
   - **Activity:** Have students match animals to their natural habitats.
   - **Assessment:** Students create a habitat diorama.

Mathematics

294. **Topic:** Measurement – Length

   - **Objective:** Learn to measure lengths using a ruler.
   - **Activity:** Measure classroom objects and record results.
   - **Assessment:** Students compare and order objects by length.

295. **Topic:** Patterns in Numbers

   - **Objective:** Recognize and create number patterns.
   - **Activity:** Create and extend number patterns with manipulatives.
   - **Assessment:** Ask students to complete an unfinished pattern.

Language Arts

296. **Topic:** Synonyms and Antonyms

   - **Objective:** Understand and identify synonyms and antonyms.
   - **Activity:** Play synonym and antonym matching games.

- **Assessment:** Students create sentences using synonyms and antonyms.

Social Studies

297. **Topic:** Maps and Directions

   - **Objective:** Learn how to read basic maps and follow directions.
   - **Activity:** Create a classroom treasure map and navigate it.
   - **Assessment:** Ask students to give directions using map symbols.

   Physical Education

298. **Topic:** Jumping and Hopping

   - **Objective:** Improve coordination and balance through jumping and hopping.
   - **Activity:** Organize relay races that include jumping and hopping.
   - **Assessment:** Observe students' form and balance during activities.

   Mathematics

307. **Topic:** Introduction to Fractions

   - **Objective:** Understand and represent basic fractions (1/2, 1/3, 1/4).
   - **Activity:** Use fruit slices or paper to show different fractions.
   - **Assessment:** Students identify and colour in fractions on worksheets.

308. **Topic:** Time – Reading Clocks

   - **Objective:** Learn to read the time on analogue clocks.

- **Activity:** Use toy clocks to practice setting and reading times.
- **Assessment:** Students draw the hands of a clock showing specific times.

Science

309. **Topic:** Weather Patterns

- **Objective:** Understand basic weather types and their characteristics.
- **Activity:** Create a weather chart for the week.
- **Assessment:** Students describe weather patterns they observe.

310. **Topic:** Animal Habitats

- **Objective:** Identify different animal habitats and their characteristics.
- **Activity:** Create a habitat diorama for an animal of choice.
- **Assessment:** Students present their dioramas and explain habitat features.

Social Studies

311. **Topic:** National Symbols

- **Objective:** Learn about national symbols and their meanings.
- **Activity:** Color and label pictures of national flags, animals, and monuments.
- **Assessment:** Discuss the significance of each symbol in class.

Language Arts

312. **Topic:** Opposites

- **Objective:** Understand and use common opposites in sentences.

- **Activity:** Match cards with opposite words.
- **Assessment:** Write sentences using pairs of opposites.

Art

313. **Topic:** Paper Collage

- **Objective:** Create an artwork using paper collage techniques.
- **Activity:** Cut shapes from coloured paper and arrange them into a picture.
- **Assessment:** Review students' final artworks for creativity and technique.

Physical Education

314. **Topic:** Team Sports – Basketball

- **Objective:** Understand basic basketball rules and practice teamwork.
- **Activity:** Conduct a friendly game of basketball.
- **Assessment:** Observe teamwork and individual skill development during the game.

Components of Effective Lesson Planning

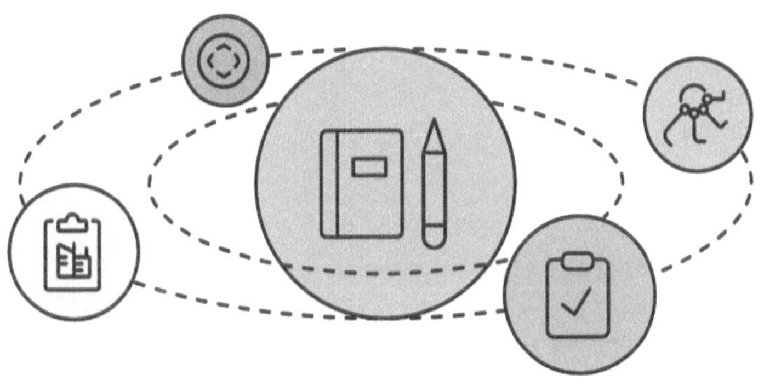

Mathematics

315. **Topic:** Simple Addition

- **Objective:** Add single-digit numbers.
- **Activity:** Use counters or visual aids to demonstrate addition.
- **Assessment:** Have students solve simple addition problems using counters.

316. **Topic:** Shapes and Patterns

- **Objective:** Recognize and classify different shapes and patterns.
- **Activity:** Draw shapes on the board and have students identify and replicate them.
- **Assessment:** Have students create their patterns using coloured paper shapes.

Science

317. **Topic:** Plants and Photosynthesis

- **Objective:** Learn how plants make their food.
- **Activity:** Observe and discuss the process of photosynthesis using a plant in the classroom.
- **Assessment:** Ask students to explain photosynthesis in their own words.

318. **Topic:** Water Cycle

- **Objective:** Understand the stages of the water cycle.
- **Activity:** Use a diagram to explain the stages (evaporation, condensation, precipitation).
- **Assessment:** Have students draw their water cycle diagram.

Social Studies

319. **Topic:** Our Community

- **Objective:** Understand the concept of a community and its roles.
- **Activity:** Discuss the different roles people play in a community (teachers, doctors, etc.).
- **Assessment:** Students create a simple community map showing different places and people.

Language Arts

320. **Topic:** Rhyming Words

- **Objective:** Identify and create rhyming words.
- **Activity:** Read a short poem or song and ask students to identify rhyming words.
- **Assessment:** Have students complete a rhyming word worksheet.

Art

321. **Topic:** Color Mixing

- **Objective:** Learn how to mix primary colours to create secondary colours.
- **Activity:** Mix colours using paint to demonstrate how new colours are made.
- **Assessment:** Have students mix their colours and create a colour wheel.

Physical Education

322. **Topic:** Obstacle Course

- **Objective:** Improve agility and coordination.

- **Activity:** Set up a simple obstacle course that requires crawling, jumping, and running.
- **Assessment:** Evaluate students' ability to complete the course and their coordination skills.

Cycle of Lesson Reflection and Adaptation

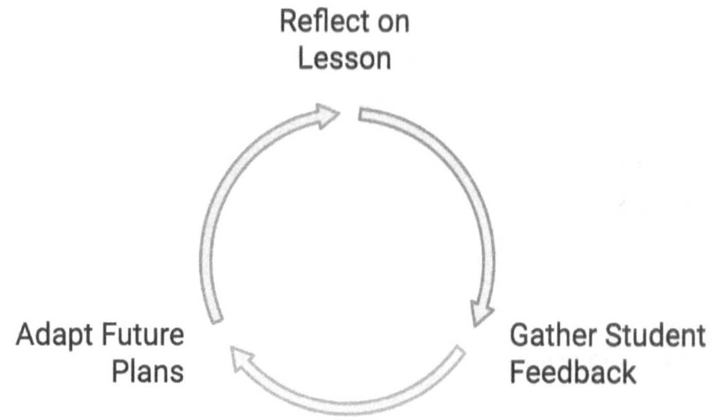

Mathematics

323. **Topic:** Measurement - Length

   - **Objective:** Introduce concepts of length and measurement units.
   - **Activity:** Use rulers to measure classroom objects.
   - **Assessment:** Have students measure different objects and record their findings.

324. **Topic:** Introduction to Multiplication

   - **Objective:** Understand basic multiplication concepts using repeated addition.
   - **Activity:** Use visual aids (e.g., groups of objects) to demonstrate multiplication.
   - **Assessment:** Provide simple multiplication problems for students to solve.

Science

325. **Topic:** Living and Non-Living Things

   - **Objective:** Understand the difference between living and non-living things.
   - **Activity:** Show pictures of various objects and ask students to classify them.
   - **Assessment:** Students list living and non-living things from their surroundings.

326. **Topic:** Simple Machines

   - **Objective:** Learn basic simple machines (lever, pulley, etc.).
   - **Activity:** Demonstrate each machine with real-life examples.
   - **Assessment:** Have students identify simple machines in the classroom.

Social Studies

327. **Topic:** Different Types of Homes Around the World

- **Objective:** Learn about various types of homes in different cultures.
- **Activity:** Show pictures of homes from different countries and discuss their characteristics.
- **Assessment:** Students create a collage of different types of homes.

Language Arts

328. **Topic:** Sentence Construction

- **Objective:** Build simple sentences using nouns, verbs, and adjectives.
- **Activity:** Create sentences with flashcards of words.
- **Assessment:** Ask students to create their sentences using given words.

Art

329. **Topic:** Nature Drawing

- **Objective:** Encourage observational skills through nature.
- **Activity:** Take students outdoors to draw plants, flowers, or trees.
- **Assessment:** Have students explain the details of their drawings.

Physical Education

330. **Topic:** Teamwork Games

- **Objective:** Understand the importance of teamwork in physical activities.

- **Activity:** Organize relay races or team-building exercises.
- **Assessment:** Evaluate students based on their ability to cooperate with teammates.

Mathematics

331. **Topic:** Fractions

- **Objective:** Introduce basic fraction concepts using visual aids.
- **Activity:** Use paper folding to show halves and quarters.
- **Assessment:** Have students identify fractions in everyday objects.

Science

332. **Topic:** Water Cycle

- **Objective:** Understand the stages of the water cycle.
- **Activity:** Create a simple diagram of the water cycle and explain it.
- **Assessment:** Ask students to draw their water cycle.

Social Studies

333. **Topic:** Transportation

- **Objective:** Learn about different modes of transportation.
- **Activity:** Show videos or images of various vehicles.
- **Assessment:** Students draw their preferred mode of transportation.

Language Arts

334. **Topic:** Rhyming Words

- **Objective:** Recognize and create rhyming words.
- **Activity:** Use a rhyming word game to encourage participation.
- **Assessment:** Students create a short rhyming poem.

Art

335. **Topic:** Color Mixing

- **Objective:** Teach the primary colours and their mixtures.
- **Activity:** Let students mix paints and create new colours.
- **Assessment:** Evaluate students' understanding of colour mixing.

Physical Education

336. **Topic:** Hand-Eye Coordination

- **Objective:** Improve hand-eye coordination with simple activities.
- **Activity:** Practice catching and throwing softballs.
- **Assessment:** Observe and provide feedback on accuracy and coordination.

Mathematics

337. **Topic:** Addition and Subtraction

- **Objective:** Reinforce essential addition and subtraction skills.
- **Activity:** Use counters or objects for hands-on practice.
- **Assessment:** Have students solve simple problems on the board.

Science

338. **Topic:** Plants and Growth

- **Objective:** Understand how plants grow and the need for sunlight and water.
- **Activity:** Plant seeds in a small container and observe over time.
- **Assessment:** Students keep a plant growth journal.

Social Studies

339. **Topic:** Community Helpers

- **Objective:** Learn about the roles of people in the community.
- **Activity:** Discuss different community helpers and their jobs.
- **Assessment:** Students create a "Community Helpers" collage.

Language Arts

340. **Topic:** Story Sequencing

- **Objective:** Understand the sequence of events in a story.
- **Activity:** Read a short story and ask students to arrange events in order.
- **Assessment:** Have students retell the story in their own words.

Art

341. **Topic:** Shape Art

- **Objective:** Teach about basic shapes and their use in art.
- **Activity:** Use cut-out shapes to create a picture.
- **Assessment:** Evaluate students' ability to identify shapes in their artwork.

Physical Education

342. **Topic:** Balancing Skills

- **Objective:** Improve balance and coordination.
- **Activity:** Set up a simple obstacle course that requires balancing.
- **Assessment:** Observe students' ability to maintain balance during the activity.

• 94 •

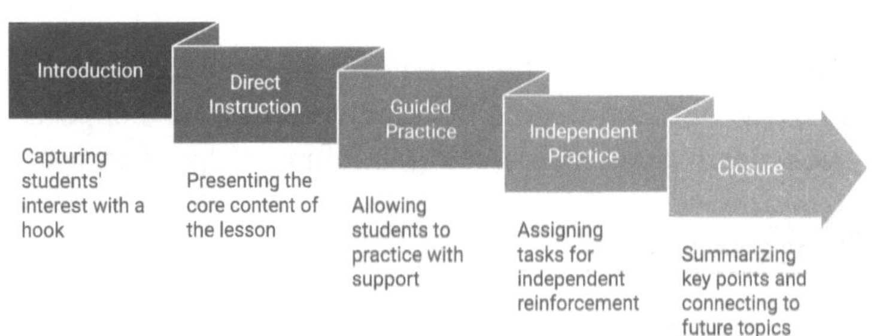

Mathematics

343. **Topic:** Place Value

   - **Objective:** Teach the concept of place value for numbers up to 1000.
   - **Activity:** Use base ten blocks to represent different numbers.
   - **Assessment:** Students identify and write numbers in expanded form.

Science

344. **Topic:** States of Matter

   - **Objective:** Understand the three states of matter (solid, liquid, gas).
   - **Activity:** Conduct simple experiments with water at different temperatures.
   - **Assessment:** Students categorize various substances based on their state.

Social Studies

345. **Topic:** National Symbols

   - **Objective:** Learn about the national symbols of the country.
   - **Activity:** Discuss the national flag, anthem, and emblem.
   - **Assessment:** Students draw or colour the national symbols.

Language Arts

346. **Topic:** Rhyming Words

   - **Objective:** Identify and create rhyming words.

- **Activity:** Read rhyming poems or stories, then have students find and make their rhymes.
- **Assessment:** Have students write a short rhyming poem.

Art

347. **Topic:** Color Mixing

- **Objective:** Teach how primary colours mix to make secondary colours.
- **Activity:** Use paints to mix colours and create a colour wheel.
- **Assessment:** Evaluate students' understanding of primary and secondary colours.

Physical Education

348. **Topic:** Throwing and Catching Skills

- **Objective:** Improve hand-eye coordination through ball skills.
- **Activity:** Practice throwing and catching with partners or against the wall.
- **Assessment:** Observe students' ability to throw and catch with accuracy.

Enhancing Lesson Planning

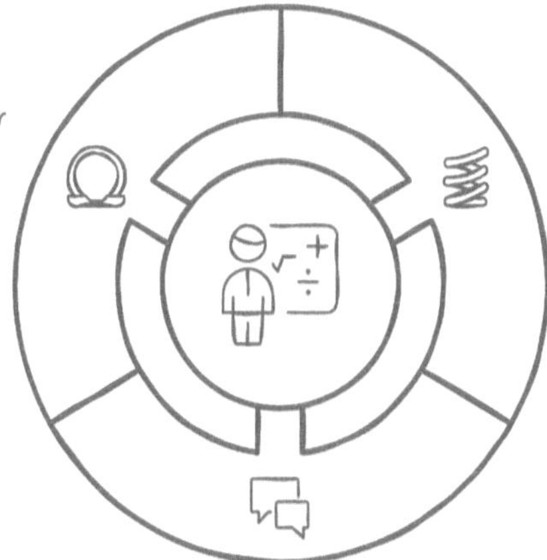

Mathematics

349. **Topic:** Time

- **Objective:** Learn to read clocks and understand time.
- **Activity:** Use analogue clocks to practice telling time.
- **Assessment:** Ask students to draw their hands on a clock to show specific times.

Science

350. **Topic:** Plant Growth

- **Objective:** Understand how plants grow and what they need to survive.
- **Activity:** Plant seeds in pots and track their growth over time.
- **Assessment:** Students record daily observations.

Social Studies

351. **Topic:** Communities

- **Objective:** Learn about different types of communities (urban, rural).
- **Activity:** Create a poster comparing urban and rural areas.
- **Assessment:** Discuss the class differences.

Language Arts

352. **Topic:** Sentence Construction

- **Objective:** Build simple and compound sentences.
- **Activity:** Use word cards to construct sentences.
- **Assessment:** Students create their sentences using given words.

Art

353. **Topic:** Shapes and Forms

- **Objective:** Identify and draw basic geometric shapes.
- **Activity:** Create a collage using different shapes.
- **Assessment:** Evaluate the use of shapes in the artwork.

Physical Education

354. **Topic:** Balancing Skills

- **Objective:** Improve balance and coordination.
- **Activity:** Set up an obstacle course that involves balancing on beams.
- **Assessment:** Observe the students' ability to complete the course without losing balance.

Effective Lesson Planning

Importance of Lesson Planning

Components of a Lesson Plan

Practical Tips for Teachers

Mathematics

355. **Topic:** Patterns in Numbers

- **Objective:** Identify and create patterns with numbers.
- **Activity:** Create a pattern with blocks or stickers and ask students to predict the following numbers.
- **Assessment:** Students write their patterns on the board.

Science

356. **Topic:** Weather Changes

- **Objective:** Understand the concept of weather and seasons.
- **Activity:** Make a weather chart and record daily observations.
- **Assessment:** Have students discuss how weather changes with the seasons.

Social Studies

357. **Topic:** National Holidays

- **Objective:** Learn about critical national holidays.
- **Activity:** Create a calendar of national holidays and discuss their significance.
- **Assessment:** Students explain the significance of a selected holiday.

Language Arts

358. **Topic:** Rhyming Words

- **Objective:** Learn to identify and create rhyming words.
- **Activity:** Rhyming word games and songs.

- **Assessment:** Ask students to come up with their own rhyming words.

Art

359. **Topic:** Colors and Emotions

- **Objective:** Understand how colors can express emotions.
- **Activity:** Paint or colour a picture to show different emotions using colours.
- **Assessment:** Evaluate students' understanding based on the emotions they express.

Physical Education

360. **Topic:** Teamwork and Cooperation

- **Objective:** Learn the value of teamwork.
- **Activity:** Group games like relay races or tug-of-war.
- **Assessment:** Observe how well students work together as a team.

Mathematics

361. **Topic:** Shapes and Geometry

- **Objective:** Learn to identify and classify shapes.
- **Activity:** Use cut-out shapes for sorting and classifying exercises.
- **Assessment:** Have students draw different shapes and name them.

Science

362. **Topic:** Plant Growth

- **Objective:** Understand the basic needs of plants.

- **Activity:** Plant a seed and track its growth over time.
- **Assessment:** Ask students to explain the life cycle of a plant.

Social Studies

363. **Topic:** Community Helpers

- **Objective:** Identify various roles within a community.
- **Activity:** Create a "Community Helpers" collage with pictures.
- **Assessment:** Students present their favourite community helper and explain their role.

Language Arts

364. **Topic:** Introduction to Sentences

- **Objective:** Learn the structure of a sentence.
- **Activity:** Rearrange words to form proper sentences.
- **Assessment:** Students write their simple sentences.

Art

365. **Topic:** Creating Collages

- **Objective:** Understand the concept of collage art.
- **Activity:** Students use magazine cutouts to create a themed collage.
- **Assessment:** Evaluate the creativity and relevance of the collage theme.

Physical Education

366. **Topic:** Healthy Habits

- **Objective:** Learn about the importance of exercise and a healthy lifestyle.
- **Activity:** Engage in exercises (e.g., stretches, jumping jacks).
- **Assessment:** Students describe how they feel before and after the exercises.

Enhance student learning through effective lesson planning.

Create enriching educational environments

Promote student success through planning.

- -

Lack of structured lesson plans

Primary teachers need guidance.

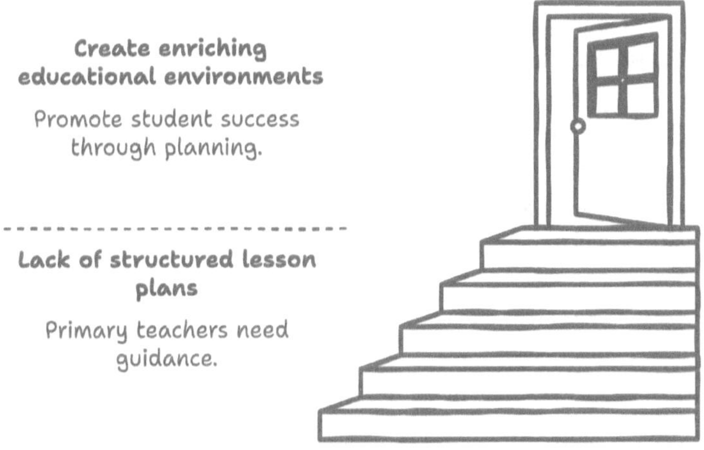

Mathematics

367. **Topic:** Counting in Hundreds

- **Objective:** Recognize numbers in hundreds.
- **Activity:** Use blocks to represent numbers and group them into hundreds.
- **Assessment:** Students write numbers up to 1000.

Science

368. **Topic:** Weather Patterns

- **Objective:** Identify weather patterns and their characteristics.
- **Activity:** Chart the weather over a week.
- **Assessment:** Students describe today's weather and match it with seasonal patterns.

Social Studies

369. **Topic:** Local Geography

- **Objective:** Understand the geography of their community.
- **Activity:** Create a simple map of their town or neighbourhood.
- **Assessment:** Identify landmarks and essential features.

Language Arts

370. **Topic:** Describing Objects

- **Objective:** Use adjectives to describe objects.
- **Activity:** Students pick and describe an object using at least five adjectives.
- **Assessment:** Write a paragraph describing a favourite object.

Art

371. **Topic:** Painting with Primary Colors

- **Objective:** Learn about primary colours and their combinations.
- **Activity:** Create a painting using only primary colours.
- **Assessment:** Students explain how they mixed colours to create new shades.

Physical Education

372. **Topic:** Balance Exercises

- **Objective:** Improve balance and coordination.
- **Activity:** Students walk along a balance beam or straight line.
- **Assessment:** Observe how well students maintain balance throughout the activity.

Mathematics

373. **Topic:** Fractions

- **Objective:** Introduce the concept of fractions.
- **Activity:** Use pizza or cake models to explain fractions visually.
- **Assessment:** Ask students to represent fractions with objects or drawings.

Science

374. **Topic:** Plant Growth

- **Objective:** Learn about the needs of plants to grow.
- **Activity:** Plant seeds in the soil and observe over time.
- **Assessment:** Record observations of plant growth and changes.

Social Studies

375. **Topic:** Community Helpers

- **Objective:** Understand different roles in a community.
- **Activity:** Invite a community helper for a talk or virtual session.
- **Assessment:** Students list what they learned from the session.

Language Arts

376. **Topic:** Rhyming Words

- **Objective:** Identify and create rhyming words.
- **Activity:** Play a rhyming word game using flashcards.
- **Assessment:** Students create their rhyming word pairs.

Art

377. **Topic:** Drawing and Shading

- **Objective:** Introduce basic shading techniques.
- **Activity:** Draw simple objects and add shading.
- **Assessment:** Evaluate the depth and accuracy of shading in student artwork.

Physical Education

378. **Topic:** Jumping Skills

- **Objective:** Improve jumping and coordination.
- **Activity:** Set up a jump obstacle course.
- **Assessment:** Measure how far students can jump or how well they perform the obstacle course.

Enhancing Lesson Planning for Primary Teachers

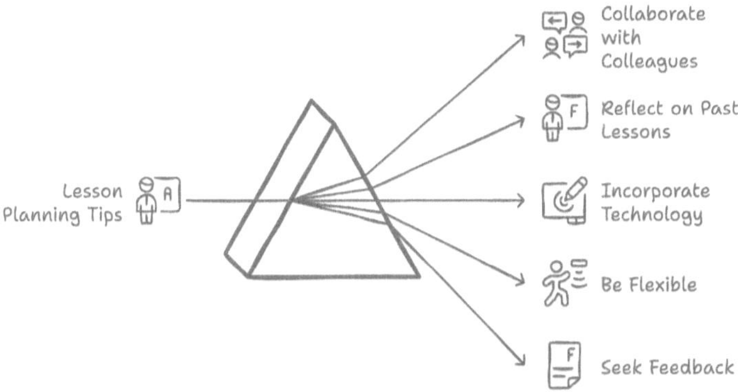

Mathematics

379. **Topic:** Time

- **Objective:** Teach how to read clocks and understand time.
- **Activity:** Use analogue clocks and ask students to set times.
- **Assessment:** Have students write the time shown on a clock.

Science

380. **Topic:** Water Cycle

- **Objective:** Understand the water cycle process.
- **Activity:** Using a bowl, plastic wrap, and a cup of water, create a simple model of the water cycle.
- **Assessment:** Ask students to label the stages of the water cycle on a diagram.

Social Studies

381. **Topic:** National Symbols

- **Objective:** Learn about national symbols (flag, emblem, etc.).
- **Activity:** Discuss the meaning of different national symbols.
- **Assessment:** Have students draw their national flag and explain its significance.

Language Arts

382. **Topic:** Parts of Speech

- **Objective:** Identify nouns, verbs, and adjectives in sentences.
- **Activity:** Have students write sentences and underline parts of speech.

- **Assessment:** Provide sentences for students to identify the parts of speech.

Art

383. **Topic:** Collage Making

    - **Objective:** Introduce collage techniques using paper and other materials.
    - **Activity:** Create a collage of a favourite scene or story.
    - **Assessment:** Evaluate creativity and use of materials.

Physical Education

384. **Topic:** Relay Races

    - **Objective:** Practice teamwork and speed through relay races.
    - **Activity:** Organize relay races with teams.
    - **Assessment:** Measure time and teamwork during the race.

English Language

385. **Topic:** Descriptive Writing

    - **Objective:** Improve skills in writing detailed descriptions.
    - **Activity:** Ask students to describe their favourite animal in detail.
    - **Assessment:** Evaluate clarity, vocabulary usage, and organization of ideas.

Science

386. **Topic:** Magnets

    - **Objective:** Understand how magnets attract and repel.

- **Activity:** Experiment with magnets and various materials to see what they attract.
- **Assessment:** Have students create a report on their findings.

Social Studies

387. **Topic:** World Continents

- **Objective:** Learn about the seven continents and their characteristics.
- **Activity:** Use a world map and label continents and oceans.
- **Assessment:** Ask students to name countries in each continent.

Mathematics

388. **Topic:** Geometry – Shapes

- **Objective:** Identify and categorize different geometric shapes.
- **Activity:** Use blocks or drawings to represent shapes.
- **Assessment:** Provide a worksheet to match shapes with their names.

Art

389. **Topic:** Watercolor Painting

- **Objective:** Teach basic watercolour techniques.
- **Activity:** Create a landscape using watercolour.
- **Assessment:** Evaluate the use of techniques such as blending and shading.

Physical Education

390. **Topic:** Jump Rope Skills

- **Objective:** Develop coordination and stamina with jump rope activities.
- **Activity:** Practice different jump rope techniques (single jump, double jump).
- **Assessment:** Track the number of successful jumps completed in a minute.

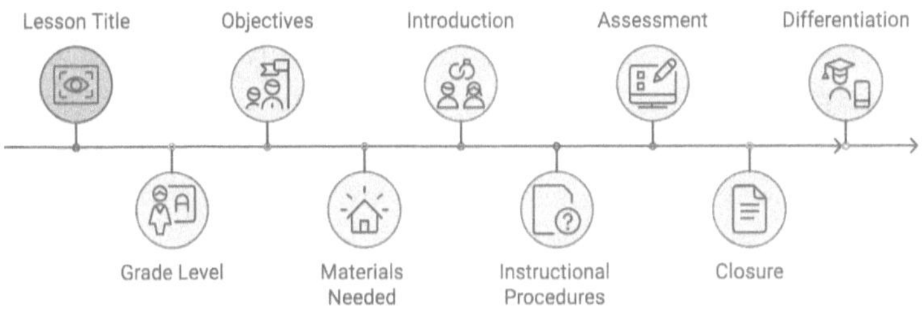

Math

391. **Topic:** Fractions

- **Objective:** Learn to identify, compare, and simplify fractions.
- **Activity:** Use fraction strips or drawings to visualize fractions.
- **Assessment:** Have students complete a worksheet comparing different fractions.

Science

392. **Topic:** Photosynthesis

- **Objective:** Understand the process of photosynthesis in plants.
- **Activity:** Conduct a simple experiment to show the effects of light on plant growth.
- **Assessment:** Ask students to explain photosynthesis in their own words.

History

393. **Topic:** Ancient Civilizations

- **Objective:** Explore the key features of ancient civilizations such as Egypt or Mesopotamia.
- **Activity:** Create a timeline of significant events in ancient history.
- **Assessment:** Quiz students on significant historical figures and inventions.

English Language Arts

394. **Topic:** Comprehension Skills

- **Objective:** Improve reading comprehension and critical thinking.
- **Activity:** Read a passage and answer related questions.
- **Assessment:** Discuss the passage to evaluate understanding and reasoning.

Art

395. **Topic:** Sculpture from Clay

- **Objective:** Learn to mould and shape clay into simple sculptures.
- **Activity:** Create a sculpture of an animal or object using air-dry clay.
- **Assessment:** Evaluate creativity, craftsmanship, and detail.

396. **Topic:** Area of Shapes

- **Objective:** Learn to calculate the area of rectangles, squares, and circles.
- **Activity:** Use graph paper to draw and measure different shapes.
- **Assessment:** Students will calculate the area of various shapes using appropriate formulas.

Science

397. **Topic:** Simple Machines

- **Objective:** Understand the six types of simple machines and their uses.
- **Activity:** Demonstrate using a lever, pulley, and ramp to lift objects.
- **Assessment:** Students will identify simple machines in everyday tools.

History

398. **Topic:** The Renaissance

- **Objective:** Explore the Renaissance's art, culture, and inventions.
- **Activity:** Research a famous Renaissance artist or inventor.
- **Assessment:** Present findings in a creative presentation (poster, slideshow).

English Language Arts

399. **Topic:** Writing Descriptive Essays

- **Objective:** Learn how to write a well-organized and descriptive essay.
- **Activity:** Brainstorm ideas and organize thoughts using a graphic organizer.
- **Assessment:** Write and submit a descriptive essay based on a chosen topic.

Physical Education

400. **Topic:** Team Sports

- **Objective:** Develop teamwork and communication through team sports.
- **Activity:** Organize a mini soccer or basketball tournament.
- **Assessment:** Evaluate students based on teamwork, communication, and skill.

Enhancing Lesson Planning Through Practical Tips

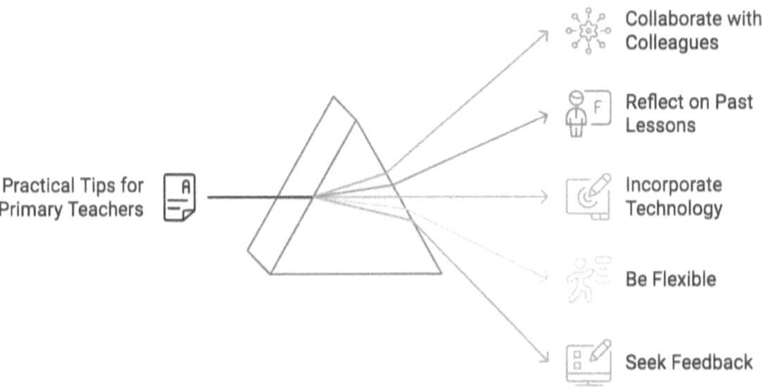

Math

401. **Topic:** Fractions

- **Objective:** Understand how to add and subtract fractions.
- **Activity:** Use visual aids like fraction bars to demonstrate adding and subtracting fractions.
- **Assessment:** Students will solve problems on paper using fraction bars for reference.

Science

402. **Topic:** The Water Cycle

- **Objective:** Learn the stages of the water cycle.
- **Activity:** Create a water cycle diagram and demonstrate with a mini experiment using a plastic bag and water.
- **Assessment:** Have students label each stage of the water cycle.

Geography

403. **Topic:** Continents and Oceans

- **Objective:** Identify and locate continents and oceans on a map.
- **Activity:** Students will label a world map and engage in a matching game of continents and oceans.
- **Assessment:** Ask students to point out specific continents and oceans on a blank map.

English Language Arts

404. **Topic:** Parts of Speech

- **Objective:** Understand and identify the different parts of speech.

- **Activity:** Use color-coded flashcards to match words with their corresponding parts of speech.
- **Assessment:** Students will write sentences and underline the parts of speech in each sentence.

Art

405. **Topic:** Color Theory

- **Objective:** Learn the primary, secondary, and tertiary colours.
- **Activity:** Mix primary colours to create secondary colours and create a colour wheel.
- **Assessment:** Students will submit a painting using at least five colours from the colour wheel.

Components of Effective Lesson Planning

Student Empowerment

Enabling active student participation

Best Practices

Strategies for optimal teaching

Teaching Experience

Enhancing educator's skills and methods

Positive Learning Environment

Creating a supportive classroom atmosphere

Student Achievement

Encouraging academic success

Math

406. **Topic:** Multiplying Decimals

- **Objective:** Learn to multiply decimals.
- **Activity:** Use grid paper to illustrate decimal multiplication and visually represent the multiplication process.
- **Assessment:** Students will solve multiple decimal multiplication problems and show work.

Science

407. **Topic:** Plant Life Cycle

- **Objective:** Understand the stages of the plant life cycle.
- **Activity:** Create a flipbook showing each stage of the plant's life cycle, from seed to full-grown plant.
- **Assessment:** Students will draw and label each stage of the plant life cycle.

History

408. **Topic:** Ancient Civilizations

- **Objective:** Learn about ancient Egyptian culture and its contributions.
- **Activity:** Students will create a timeline of significant events in ancient Egypt.
- **Assessment:** Students will write a paragraph explaining one significant achievement of ancient Egypt.

Social Studies

409. **Topic:** Community Helpers

- **Objective:** Understand the roles and importance of community helpers.
- **Activity:** Have students role-play as various community helpers and act out a day in their lives.
- **Assessment:** Students will draw their favourite community helper and explain their job.

Physical Education

410. **Topic:** Team Sports

- **Objective:** Learn the basic rules of a team sport like soccer.
- **Activity:** Set up a mini-soccer game where students practice passing, dribbling, and shooting.
- **Assessment:** Observe students' participation and teamwork during the game.

Lesson Reflection and Improvement Process

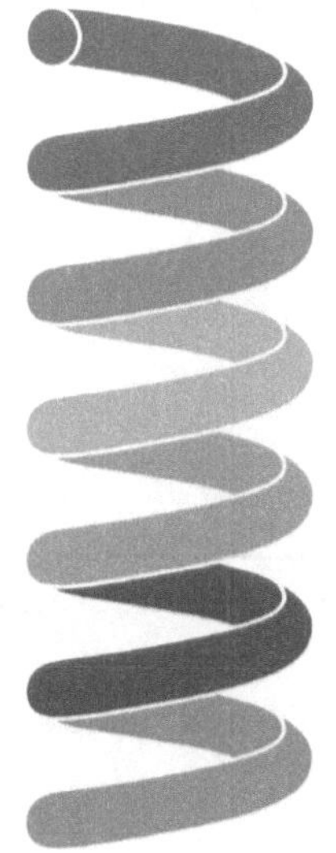

 Conduct Lesson

 Reflect on Lesson

 Gather Feedback

 Consider Perspectives

 Revise Lesson Plan

 Implement Revised Plan

Art

411. **Topic:** Abstract Art

- **Objective:** Understand the basics of abstract art and create an abstract piece.
- **Activity:** Introduce famous abstract artists and ask students to create their artwork using various colours and shapes.
- **Assessment:** Evaluate based on creativity and understanding of abstract concepts.

Music

412. **Topic:** Rhythm and Beats

- **Objective:** Understand the concept of rhythm in music.
- **Activity:** Use clapping and simple percussion instruments to demonstrate different rhythms.
- **Assessment:** Students will perform their rhythm patterns in small groups.

Science

413. **Topic:** States of Matter

- **Objective:** Identify and describe the different states of matter.
- **Activity:** Use ice, water, and steam to demonstrate the changes in states of matter.
- **Assessment:** Students will complete a worksheet categorizing substances as solid, liquid, or gas.

Geography

414. **Topic:** Continents and Oceans

- **Objective:** Learn about the seven continents and five oceans.
- **Activity:** Have students label a world map and memorize the continents and oceans.
- **Assessment:** Quiz students on the locations of continents and oceans.

Language Arts

415. **Topic:** Story Writing

- **Objective:** Learn the structure of a story.
- **Activity:** Students will write their own short stories using a given theme.
- **Assessment:** Review their writing for creativity, structure, and grammar.

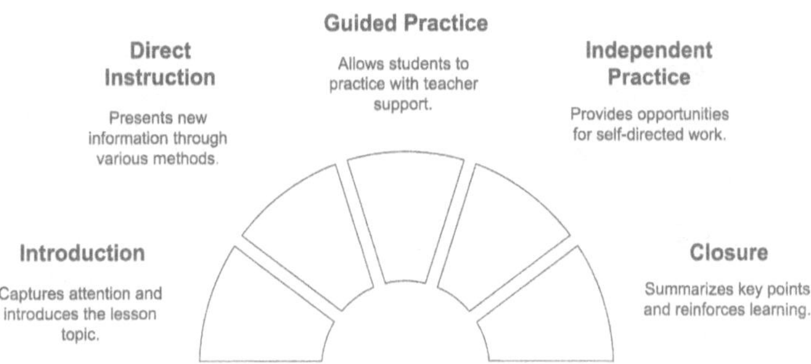

History

416. **Topic:** Ancient Civilizations

- **Objective:** Understand the culture, achievements, and legacy of ancient civilizations.
- **Activity:** Create a timeline of significant events from one civilization, such as Ancient Egypt or Mesopotamia.
- **Assessment:** Students present their timelines and discuss key historical moments.

Physical Education

417. **Topic:** Team Sports: Soccer

- **Objective:** Learn the basic rules and techniques of soccer.
- **Activity:** Conduct drills for passing, dribbling, and shooting, followed by a mini-match.
- **Assessment:** Observe teamwork, skill execution, and game strategies.

Math

418. **Topic:** Fractions

- **Objective:** Understand the concept and comparison of fractions.
- **Activity:** Use fraction strips or pie charts to demonstrate various fractions.
- **Assessment:** Worksheets with fraction problems for comparison and simplification.

Drama

419. **Topic:** Improvisation

- **Objective:** Develop creativity and quick thinking through improvisation.
- **Activity:** Provide students with a scenario and have them improvise a short scene.
- **Assessment:** Evaluate creativity, confidence, and expression during performances.

Technology

420. **Topic:** Basic Computer Skills

- **Objective:** Learn to use essential computer functions like typing and navigating programs.
- **Activity:** Complete exercises in word processing and spreadsheet programs.
- **Assessment:** Test their ability to format a document or create a simple spreadsheet.

Music

421. **Topic:** Understanding Rhythm

- **Objective:** Learn to identify and practice different rhythms.
- **Activity:** Clap with different time signatures like 4/4, 3/4, and 6/8.
- **Assessment:** Perform a short rhythm exercise in front of the class.

Social Studies

422. **Topic:** Geography of Continents

- **Objective:** Understand the geographical features of different continents.

- **Activity:** Create a world map and label countries, mountains, rivers, etc.
- **Assessment:** Quiz on significant continents and their features.

Science

423. **Topic:** Plant Growth

- **Objective:** Learn about the conditions necessary for plant growth.
- **Activity:** Plant seeds and observe their growth under different conditions (light, water, etc.).
- **Assessment:** Document observations and make conclusions.

Art

424. **Topic:** Watercolor Techniques

- **Objective:** Explore various watercolour techniques, such as wet-on-wet and wet-on-dry.
- **Activity:** Create a painting using these techniques.
- **Assessment:** Evaluate the use of technique and creativity in the final artwork.

Language Arts

425. **Topic:** Writing a Short Story

- **Objective:** Learn the elements of a short story: character, setting, plot, conflict, and resolution.
- **Activity:** Write a short story based on a prompt or personal experience.
- **Assessment:** Review the structure, creativity, and grammar of the story.

Steps to Effective Lesson Planning

Know Your Students

Understand students' diverse backgrounds and learning styles to tailor the lesson plan effectively.

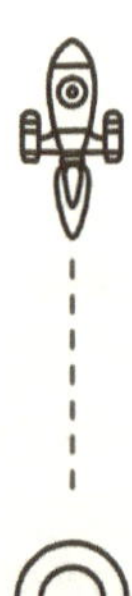

Define Learning Objectives

Establish specific, measurable, achievable, relevant, and time-bound objectives to guide the lesson.

Physical Education

426. **Topic:** Basic Fitness Training

- **Objective:** Learn the importance of physical fitness.
- **Activity:** Engage in warm-up exercises followed by short sprints and strength training exercises.
- **Assessment:** Monitor the student's progress through a fitness test.

Science

427. **Topic:** Simple Machines

- **Objective:** Identify and understand simple machines like levers, pulleys, and inclined planes.
- **Activity:** Build a simple machine using everyday objects.
- **Assessment:** Discuss the function and benefits of the machine created.

Math

428. **Topic:** Understanding Fractions

- **Objective:** Learn how to recognize and work with fractions.
- **Activity:** Use visual aids like fraction charts and divide objects into fractional parts.
- **Assessment:** Solve problems using fractions.

History

429. **Topic:** The Industrial Revolution

- **Objective:** Learn about the key events and impacts of the Industrial Revolution.

- **Activity:** Create a timeline of significant events and inventions during this period.
- **Assessment:** Discuss the effects of the revolution on modern society.

Language Arts

430. **Topic:** Vocabulary Building

- **Objective:** Enhance vocabulary through word games and exercises.
- **Activity:** Play a word association game and have students create sentences using new words.
- **Assessment:** Have students write a paragraph using the new vocabulary.

Geography

431. **Topic:** Understanding Maps and Globes

- **Objective:** Learn to read maps and understand the concept of continents, countries, and oceans.
- **Activity:** Use physical maps to locate and identify various geographical features.
- **Assessment:** Complete a worksheet identifying different countries and continents on a map.

Art

432. **Topic:** Introduction to Watercolor Painting

- **Objective:** Introduce basic watercolor techniques.
- **Activity:** Demonstrate simple techniques and let students paint a nature scene.

- **Assessment:** Evaluate creativity, use of colour, and application of watercolour techniques.

Music

433. **Topic:** Introduction to Rhythm

- **Objective:** Teach the basics of rhythm and timing.
- **Activity:** Use clapping exercises or rhythm instruments to practice different beats.
- **Assessment:** Have students demonstrate understanding by playing rhythms on instruments.

Social Studies

434. **Topic:** Government and Leadership

- **Objective:** Learn about different forms of government.
- **Activity:** Hold a mock election where students create their political party and campaign.
- **Assessment:** Assess participation and understanding through class discussion.

Technology

435. **Topic:** Basic Coding and Programming

- **Objective:** Introduce students to the concepts of coding and programming logic.
- **Activity:** Use simple coding platforms like Scratch to teach students to create basic programs.
- **Assessment:** Evaluate the programs students create for functionality and creativity.

Best Practices in Lesson Planning

Science

436. **Topic:** Exploring the Water Cycle

- **Objective:** Understand the stages of the water cycle.
- **Activity:** Create a simple water cycle model using plastic wrap and water.
- **Assessment:** Have students describe the process in their own words and explain the stages.

Math

437. **Topic:** Basic Multiplication Strategies

- **Objective:** Learn multiplication facts using visual aids.
- **Activity:** Use number lines or group objects to demonstrate multiplication.
- **Assessment:** Complete a worksheet with multiplication problems.

Language Arts

438. **Topic:** Writing a Personal Narrative

- **Objective:** Learn how to structure and write a personal story.
- **Activity:** Write a story about a memorable experience, focusing on sequencing events.
- **Assessment:** Review the narrative for clarity, structure, and creativity.

History

439. **Topic:** Ancient Civilizations

- **Objective:** Understand key features of early civilizations.

- **Activity:** Research and present on different ancient civilizations, focusing on culture, government, and innovations.
- **Assessment:** Create a poster or presentation summarizing their findings.

Physical Education

440. **Topic:** Teamwork and Cooperation in Sports

- **Objective:** Teach students the importance of teamwork.
- **Activity:** Organize cooperative games that require team strategies.
- **Assessment:** Observe teamwork and sportsmanship during activities.

Art

441. **Topic:** Color Mixing and Theory

- **Objective:** Teach students about primary and secondary colours.
- **Activity:** Mix primary colours to create secondary ones, then create a colourful painting using those colours.
- **Assessment:** Evaluate their use of colour mixing and creativity in their artwork.

Geography

442. **Topic:** Exploring Continents and Oceans

- **Objective:** Introduce students to the seven continents and five oceans.
- **Activity:** Use a world map to label continents and oceans.
- **Assessment:** Students will label a blank map correctly.

Music

443. **Topic:** Introduction to Musical Instruments

- **Objective:** Understand the different types of musical instruments.
- **Activity:** Show and tell session of various musical instruments.
- **Assessment:** Have students identify instruments by sound or image.

Social Studies

444. **Topic:** Government and Citizenship

- **Objective:** Understand a government's basic structure and the citizen's role.
- **Activity:** Create a simple class constitution and vote on classroom rules.
- **Assessment:** Assess student participation and understanding of government functions.

Computer Science

445. **Topic:** Basic Coding with Scratch

- **Objective:** Introduce the concept of coding to students using Scratch.
- **Activity:** Create a simple animated story or game using Scratch blocks.
- **Assessment:** Evaluate the creativity and accuracy of the students' coding projects.

Effective Lesson Planning

Importance of Lesson Planning 

 Components of a Lesson Plan

Practical Tips for Teachers 

Math

446. **Topic:** Introduction to Fractions

- **Objective:** Teach students to identify and understand fractions.
- **Activity:** Use visual aids like fraction circles to represent fractions and their parts.
- **Assessment:** Have students identify and match fractions to images.

Science

447. **Topic:** Water Cycle

- **Objective:** Understand the process of the water cycle.
- **Activity:** Create a jar's water cycle model using heat and condensation.
- **Assessment:** Ask students to describe the stages of the water cycle.

History

448. **Topic:** The Civil War

- **Objective:** Learn about the causes and impact of the Civil War.
- **Activity:** Create a timeline of key events during the Civil War.
- **Assessment:** Students write a short reflection on one key event.

Physical Education

449. **Topic:** Team Sports and Cooperation

- **Objective:** Emphasize teamwork and cooperation in sports.
- **Activity:** Play a team-based game like soccer or relay races.
- **Assessment:** Observe students' teamwork and communication during the game.

Literature

450. **Topic:** Character Analysis in a Short Story

- **Objective:** Develop skills in analyzing literary characters.
- **Activity:** Have students read a short story and complete a character analysis worksheet.
- **Assessment:** Evaluate students' ability to provide evidence for their character traits.

Geography

451. **Topic:** Maps and Globes

- **Objective:** Understand the use and importance of maps and globes.
- **Activity:** Have students label continents and oceans on a world map.
- **Assessment:** Ask students to complete a map quiz.

Art

452. **Topic:** Color Theory

- **Objective:** Learn about primary, secondary, and tertiary colours.
- **Activity:** Have students mix primary colours to create secondary colours.
- **Assessment:** Evaluate students' ability to match colours and identify colour mixes.

Social Studies

453. **Topic:** Community Helpers

- **Objective:** Learn about different roles in the community.
- **Activity:** Invite a local community helper to speak with the class.
- **Assessment:** Have students create a poster showcasing a community helper.

Language Arts

454. **Topic:** Creative Writing

- **Objective:** Develop imaginative writing skills.
- **Activity:** Have students write a short story with a beginning, middle, and end.
- **Assessment:** Review students' stories for creativity and structure.

Math

455. **Topic:** Multiplication Word Problems

- **Objective:** Apply multiplication to real-world scenarios.

- **Activity:** Provide word problems for students to solve using multiplication.
- **Assessment:** Check the accuracy and process used in solving the problems

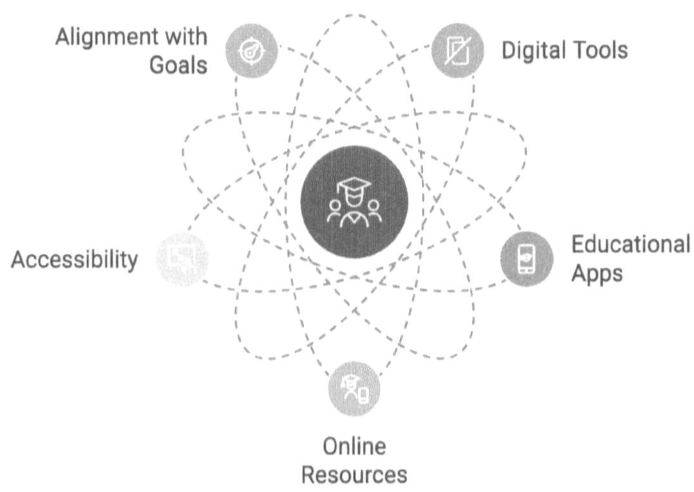

Science

456. **Topic:** States of Matter

- **Objective:** Learn the three states of matter: solid, liquid, and gas.
- **Activity:** Conduct simple experiments to observe state changes, like melting ice or boiling water.
- **Assessment:** Ask students to classify different objects based on their state at room temperature.

Math

457. **Topic:** Addition and Subtraction

- **Objective:** Practice essential addition and subtraction skills.
- **Activity:** Create flashcards with addition and subtraction problems.
- **Assessment:** Have students solve the problems on the board and explain their reasoning.

Art

458. **Topic:** Drawing with Shapes

- **Objective:** Teach students to create drawings using basic shapes.
- **Activity:** Guide students to create animals or objects using circles, squares, and triangles.
- **Assessment:** Evaluate students' ability to identify and use shapes in their drawings.

Social Studies

459. **Topic:** Ancient Civilizations

- **Objective:** Learn about the achievements of ancient civilizations.

- **Activity:** Have students create a timeline of key events from a chosen civilization.
- **Assessment:** Test students on essential facts and milestones from the civilization studied.

Language Arts

460. **Topic:** Sentence Structure

- **Objective:** Understand and practice proper sentence formation.
- **Activity:** Provide incomplete sentences for students to complete.
- **Assessment:** Review completed sentences for correct structure and grammar.

Science

461. **Topic:** Forces and Motion

- **Objective:** Understand the concept of force and how it affects motion.
- **Activity:** Use toy cars to demonstrate the effects of different forces (push, pull, gravity).
- **Assessment:** Have students predict how different forces affect motion and verify with experiments.

Math

462. **Topic:** Geometry - Shapes and Angles

- **Objective:** Learn to identify and measure angles.
- **Activity:** Provide a protractor and ask students to measure angles in different shapes.
- **Assessment:** Test students' ability to identify and measure various angles.

Art

463. **Topic:** Color Mixing

- **Objective:** Understand primary, secondary, and tertiary colours.
- **Activity:** Mix primary colours to create secondary colours.
- **Assessment:** Review students' colour creation and understanding of the colour wheel.

Social Studies

464. **Topic:** Geography of the Continents

- **Objective:** Identify and locate continents on a map.
- **Activity:** Provide a world map and ask students to label the continents.
- **Assessment:** Check students' map labelling accuracy.

Language Arts

465. **Topic:** Reading Comprehension

- **Objective:** Improve students' ability to understand and analyze texts.
- **Activity:** Have students read a passage and answer comprehension questions.
- **Assessment:** Evaluate responses based on an understanding of the text.

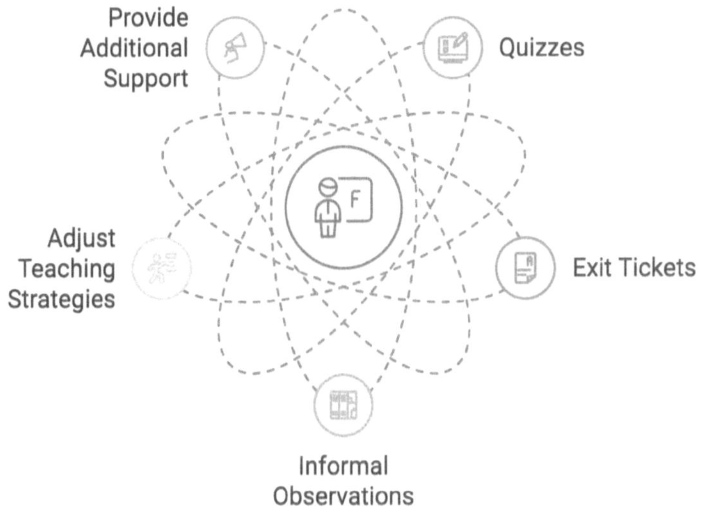

Enhancing Teaching with Formative Assessments
Provide Additional Support
Quizzes
Adjust Teaching Strategies
Exit Tickets
Informal Observations

Science

466. **Topic:** Plant Growth

   - **Objective:** Understand the basic requirements for plant growth.
   - **Activity:** Have students plant seeds in small containers and track their growth over several weeks.
   - **Assessment:** Observe and document plant growth, noting height and leaf formation changes.

Math

467. **Topic:** Division with Remainders

   - **Objective:** Practice division of more significant numbers with remainders.
   - **Activity:** Provide problems involving division with remainders and let students solve them using manipulatives or division charts.
   - **Assessment:** Review student responses to ensure they can calculate remainders correctly.

Art

468. **Topic:** Texture Exploration

   - **Objective:** Explore different textures through art.
   - **Activity:** Use textured materials (e.g., fabric, sandpaper) for students to create a textured art piece.
   - **Assessment:** Evaluate the use of different textures in the artwork.

Social Studies

469. **Topic:** Early Civilizations

- **Objective:** Learn about the key characteristics of early civilizations.
- **Activity:** Show students artefacts or pictures and ask them to identify what civilization they belong to.
- **Assessment:** Have students write a brief report on one early civilization.

Language Arts

470. **Topic:** Parts of Speech

- **Objective:** Teach students about nouns, verbs, and adjectives.
- **Activity:** Have students create sentences using different parts of speech and identify each part in the sentence.
- **Assessment:** Test students' ability to label parts of speech in sentences.

Science

471. **Topic:** Water Cycle

- **Objective:** Understand the process of the water cycle.
- **Activity:** Create a simple model of the water cycle using a plastic bag and water.
- **Assessment:** Ask students to label each stage of the water cycle and explain the process.

Math

472. **Topic:** Fractions

- **Objective:** Introduce fractions and their parts.
- **Activity:** Use paper plates to visually show fractions, cutting them into halves, thirds, and fourths.

- **Assessment:** Have students write fractions based on the parts of their paper plate.

Art

473. **Topic:** Color Mixing

- **Objective:** Learn how to mix primary colours to create secondary colours.
- **Activity:** Provide primary-coloured paints and let students mix them to create new colours.
- **Assessment:** Check for understanding by having students name the secondary colours they've created.

Social Studies

474. **Topic:** Local History

- **Objective:** Investigate the history of the local community.
- **Activity:** Take a walking tour of a nearby historical site and discuss its significance.
- **Assessment:** Have students write a short report on what they learned about the site.

Language Arts

475. **Topic:** Storytelling

- **Objective:** Encourage creativity through storytelling.
- **Activity:** Ask students to create short stories using a picture prompt.
- **Assessment:** Assess their ability to structure a story with a beginning, middle, and end.

Positive Learning Environment Outcomes

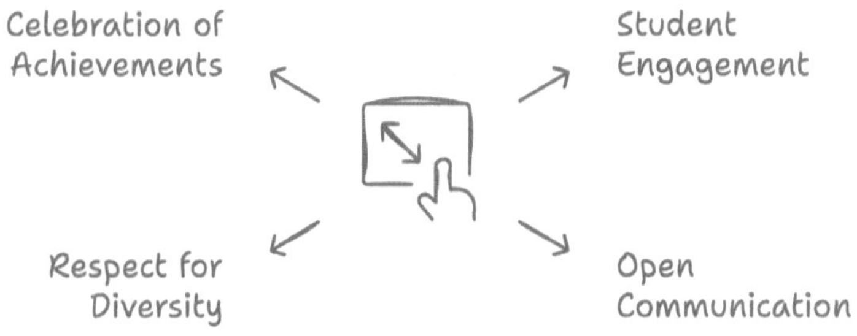

476. **Topic:** Plant Growth

- **Objective:** Understand the factors affecting plant growth.
- **Activity:** Plant seeds in small cups and observe their growth over weeks, varying light and water.
- **Assessment:** Have students record the growth and discuss which factors helped the plants grow best.

Math

477. **Topic:** Addition and Subtraction

- **Objective:** Master essential addition and subtraction skills.
- **Activity:** Use counters or manipulatives to demonstrate addition and subtraction visually.
- **Assessment:** Provide simple problems for students to solve using counters.

Art

478. **Topic:** Sculpture

- **Objective:** Introduce the concept of three-dimensional art.
- **Activity:** Create sculptures using clay or playdough.
- **Assessment:** Ask students to explain the process and techniques they used in their sculpture.

Social Studies

479. **Topic:** World Maps

- **Objective:** Learn to identify continents, oceans, and countries.
- **Activity:** Use a world map and have students label countries and oceans.

- **Assessment:** Test students on their knowledge of the map using flashcards.

Language Arts

480. **Topic:** Poetry

  - **Objective:** Understand basic poetic structures.
  - **Activity:** Read a short poem together and analyze its rhyme scheme.
  - **Assessment:** Have students write their short poem with a specific rhyme pattern.

Math

481. **Topic:** Shapes and Geometry

  - **Objective:** Learn to identify and categorize different shapes.
  - **Activity:** Provide a set of shapes for students to sort into categories (2D, 3D).
  - **Assessment:** Have students draw and label their favourite shapes on paper.

Science

482. **Topic:** Animal Habitats

  - **Objective:** Understand where animals live and why.
  - **Activity:** Show pictures of animals in their natural habitats and discuss.
  - **Assessment:** Have students create a poster of their favourite animal and its habitat.

Social Studies

483. **Topic:** Local Government

- **Objective:** Learn about the roles of local government.
- **Activity:** Discuss the role of the mayor, councillors, etc., in a town.
- **Assessment:** Role-play a town council meeting.

Language Arts

484. **Topic:** Sentence Structure

- **Objective:** Learn about subject-verb-object sentence structure.
- **Activity:** Have students form sentences from word cards.
- **Assessment:** Ask students to identify subjects, verbs, and objects in sentences.

Art

485. **Topic:** Color Mixing

- **Objective:** Learn primary and secondary colours.
- **Activity:** Mix paints to create new colours.
- **Assessment:** Have students demonstrate the creation of secondary colours from primary ones.

How to enhance student engagement in learning?

Incorporate Gamification

Makes learning fun and competitive through quizzes and rewards.

Encourage Student Choice

Increases investment by allowing students to choose projects or assessment methods.

Math

486. **Topic:** Counting Money

- **Objective:** Learn to identify coins and bills and practice simple addition and subtraction with money.
- **Activity:** Set up a mock store where students use play money to "buy" and "sell" items.
- **Assessment:** Have students calculate how much change they should receive after a purchase.

Science

487. **Topic:** Simple Machines

- **Objective:** Learn about levers, pulleys, and inclined planes.
- **Activity:** Build simple machines with classroom materials.
- **Assessment:** Have students describe how their machine works and what it does.

Social Studies

488. **Topic:** Geography of Continents

- **Objective:** Learn about the continents and their locations.
- **Activity:** Use a world map to quiz students on where each continent is.
- **Assessment:** Ask students to colour the continents on a blank map.

Language Arts

489. **Topic:** Rhyming Words

- **Objective:** Identify and create rhyming words.

- **Activity:** Play a rhyming word game where students find pairs of words that rhyme.
- **Assessment:** Have students write their rhyming couplets.

Art

490. **Topic:** Collage Art

- **Objective:** Explore texture and composition in art.
- **Activity:** Provide materials like paper, fabric, and magazine cutouts for students to create a collage.
- **Assessment:** Discuss with students the textures and elements they used in their artwork.

Math

491. **Topic:** Multiplication Facts

- **Objective:** Reinforce multiplication tables from 1 to 10.
- **Activity:** Have students play a multiplication bingo game with the answers to multiplication problems.
- **Assessment:** Ask students to solve a set of problems individually.

Science

492. **Topic:** Plant Growth

- **Objective:** Learn how plants grow and the conditions needed for plant growth.
- **Activity:** Plant seeds in cups and track their growth over several weeks.
- **Assessment:** Have students draw the plant at different stages of growth.

Social Studies

493. **Topic:** Local Communities

- **Objective:** Understand the structure and roles of a local community.
- **Activity:** Have students create a map of their local community, marking essential places (e.g., school, post office).
- **Assessment:** Discuss the roles of different community members with students.

Language Arts

494. **Topic:** Short Stories

- **Objective:** Identify the elements of a short story (beginning, middle, end).
- **Activity:** Read a short story and have students identify these key elements.
- **Assessment:** Ask students to write their own short story with a clear beginning, middle, and end.

Art

495. **Topic:** Color Mixing

- **Objective:** Understand primary and secondary colours.
- **Activity:** Provide students with primary colours and have them mix to create secondary colours.
- **Assessment:** Have students create art using their newly mixed colours.

Engaging Students Through Dynamic Lesson Planning

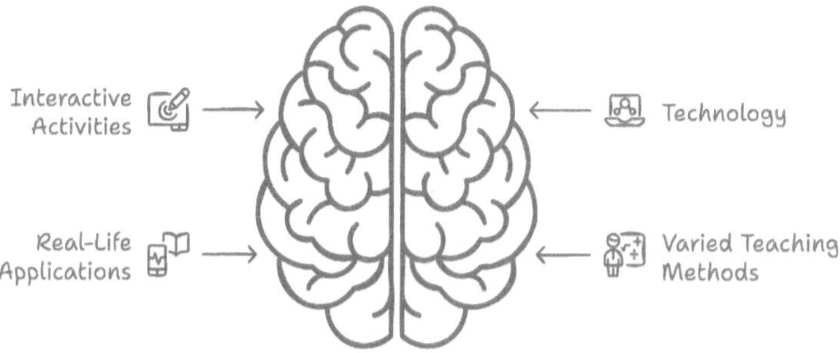

Math

496. **Topic:** Time Telling

- **Objective:** Understand how to read analogue and digital clocks.
- **Activity:** Provide clock face worksheets where students draw their hands to show a specific time.
- **Assessment:** Have students answer time-related questions and show the correct time on a clock.

Science

497. **Topic:** Water Cycle

- **Objective:** Understand the stages of the water cycle.
- **Activity:** Use a water cycle model to show evaporation, condensation, and precipitation.
- **Assessment:** Ask students to draw the water cycle and explain each stage.

Social Studies

498. **Topic:** Cultural Traditions

- **Objective:** Explore and appreciate diverse cultural traditions.
- **Activity:** Have students research and present a cultural tradition to the class.
- **Assessment:** Evaluate students' presentation skills and understanding of the tradition.

Language Arts

499. **Topic:** Adjectives

- **Objective:** Understand and use adjectives in sentences.

- **Activity**: Provide students with a list of nouns and have them describe them with adjectives.
- **Assessment**: Ask students to write sentences using at least three adjectives.

Art

500. **Topic**: Sculpture

- **Objective**: Create a sculpture using clay or other materials.
- **Activity**: Guide students to design and shape a sculpture based on a theme.
- **Assessment**: Assess the creativity, effort, and execution of the sculpture.

These lesson plans can help foster creativity, critical thinking, and hands-on learning in various subjects.

THREE

TOP 25 TIPS TO LESSON PLANNING

Planning lessons for young children is gratifying and demanding. These tactics can help educators inspire a passion for learning and help young students succeed.

Effective Lesson Planning

Reflection and Adaptation

Continuously improving lessons based on feedback and outcomes.

Understanding Students

Tailoring lessons to individual needs and interests.

Positive Environment

Creating a supportive and encouraging classroom atmosphere.

Clear Objectives

Setting specific, measurable goals for each lesson.

Engaging Methods

Using varied, interactive techniques to maintain interest.

1. Know Your Students

Understanding student requirements, interests, and development phases helps you personalise classes.

2. Set Clear Goals

Set quantifiable learning goals for each lesson to plan and evaluate student progress.

3. Simplify

Avoid complicated directions and use simple language and concepts for young children.

4. Include Play

Play-based learning makes education fun and accessible for young children.

5. Use Visual Aids

Use images, charts, and objects to improve comprehension and recall.

6. Interact

Engage kids with hands-on activities, group work, and debates.

7. Change Teaching Methods

To accommodate multiple learning styles, use narrative, music, and dance.

8. Establish Routine

To make kids feel safe and prepared, keep instruction regular.

9. Move in

Include physical exercises to help kids focus and release energy during classes.

10. Use Tech Wisely

Use age-appropriate apps and movies to increase learning.

11. Create a Positive Environment

Make your classroom a secure space for kids to express themselves.

12. Be Patient

Allow young children more time to process and react to questions.

13. Encourage Creativity

Encourage art, music, and imaginative play.

14. Offer Choices

Allow youngsters to choose their learning activities to foster autonomy and involvement.

15. Tell Stories

Explain lessons with anecdotes to make abstract topics familiar.

16. Evaluate Understanding

Use informal assessments like observations and discussions to check student comprehension throughout the course.

17. Work with Others

Sharing ideas and resources with other teachers improves lesson planning and execution.

18. Involve Families

Share lesson plans and recommend home activities to engage parents.

19. Be Flexible

Adapt your lesson plans to the kids' responses and interests.

20. Transition Plan

Smooth transitions between events keep people engaged and reduce disturbances.

21. Repeat

Young children benefit from hearing and practising concepts several times.

22. Celebrate Success

Celebrate minor victories to inspire children to learn.

23. Practice Social Skills

Encourage teamwork, sharing, and communication to improve

social skills.

24. Consider Lessons

After each lesson, evaluate what succeeded and what may be improved for future preparation.

25. Enjoy Method

Have fun while teaching—your enthusiasm will motivate your students.

Dear Teachers, Kindly Follow these tips to develop engaging and successful classes that meet the requirements of little children, creating a positive learning environment that fosters growth and curiosity.

About The Author

Dheeraj Mehrotra, a white and a yellow belt in SIX SIGMA, a Certified NLP Business Diploma holder, is an Educational Innovator, Author with expertise in Six Sigma In Education, Academic Audits, Neuro-Linguistic Programming (NLP), Total Quality Management In Education, an Experiential Educator, a CBSE Resource towards School Assessment (SQAA), CCE, JIT, Five S, and KAIZEN. He has authored over 100 books on computer science, AI, digital body language, NLP, quality circles, school management, classroom effectiveness, and safety and security. A former Principal at De Indian Public School, New Delhi, (INDIA), NPS International School, Guwahati, Kunwar's Global School, Lucknow and an Education Officer at GEMS, Gurgaon, with ample teaching experience of over Three Decades, he is a certified Trainer for Quality Circles/ TQM in Education and QCI Standards for School Accreditation/ School Audits and Management. He has also been honoured with the President of India's National Teacher Award in 2006 and the Best Science Teacher State Award (By the Ministry of Science and Technology, State of UP), among others. He has published over 100 books and developed 150 FREE EDUCATIONAL MOBILE Apps for the Google Play Store exclusively for Teachers, Students, and Parents. This work has been recognised by the LIMCA BOOK OF RECORDS and INDIA BOOK OF RECORDS as the only Indian to draw that feast. As a premium UDEMY Instructor, he has developed over 500 courses and caters to over 8 Lakh students from 180 countries. As a founder and president of the IoT Society of India, he also promotes Technology Globally. Dr Mehrotra is presently engaged as a REGIONAL HEAD of the GEMS EDUCATION India Region.

www.authordheerajmehrotra.com

Books By The Same Author

Scan Here